Charla Corn Barrett

LETTERS TO MY DAUGHTER

Timeless Lessons from the Bible's
Most Remarkable Women

Letters to My Daughter
© 2021 by Charla Corn Barrett

Published by Grafo House Publishing
Guadalajara, Jalisco, Mexico
In association with Jaquith Creataive
Bothell, Washington, USA

Hardbound ISBN 978-1-949791-50-1
Paperback ISBN 978-1-949791-47-1
Ebook ISBN 978-1-949791-48-8

Cover design and book layout by Ignacio Huizar
www.nachohuizar.com

Also available in audiobook format.
For more information or to contact the author, visit charlacorn.com.

Printed in the United States of America
24 23 22 21   1 2 3 4

PRAISE FOR LETTERS TO MY DAUGHTER

In a time when we long for mentors to show us how to navigate all the twists and turns, joys and struggles, uncertainties and victories of our lives as women, Charla Corn Barrett shows us the timeless lessons and contemporary applications of the mentors readily available to us through the women of the Bible. Weaving together her own life experiences and powerful observations on the scriptural female generations who paved the way, Charla captures the wisdom we need to inspire, teach, and guide us into our tomorrows."

—Julie Lyles Carr, best-selling author, national speaker, and *allmomdoes* podcast host

I love how Charla Corn Barrett has the heart to inspire young women and fervently share her memoir with the next generation. Letters to my Daughter is an insightful account full of narratives that reveal essential life lessons and spur all of us toward all that God has for us. Charla's passion for sharing and passing it on is refreshing.

—Thelisa E. Nutt, Ph.D., LPC

To my daughter, Blakelyn.
You've taught me more than I'll ever teach you.
May you always let God's light burst out of you
and pour over every person you encounter in this life.

CONTENTS

INTRODUCTION

THIS BOOK HAS SURPRISED ME EVERY STEP OF THE WAY. It didn't even start out as a book, to be honest. It was simply a collection of thoughts I wanted to share with my young daughter. But the more I wrote, the more it grew until it became the volume you're holding in your hands or listening to as an audiobook.

My daughter Blakelyn is only eight years old now. But time flies, as we all know. These letters are not just for my daughter now, but for every age of her life, and they are for daughters everywhere, and they are for mothers of daughters, and they are for all of God's daughters. The truths of the Bible are timeless, after all, and the legendary women whose stories are found in its pages still speak to us today.

Before we begin, I'd like to share the heart behind this project. It started in December 2008, long before Blakelyn was even born. I was still in my twenties. Stepping on stage with my guitar hanging around my neck felt like home to me. Whether it was a smoky bar with fifty people or a festival in a field with thousands, the stage is where I felt most alive.

The life of an aspiring country music singer isn't as glamorous as it sounds, though. Music was my career, which meant couch surfing was, too. I crashed on my older brother's couch in Austin, my sister's couch in Midland, and my younger brother's couch in Dallas. The highway was my home, my family, and my best friend. I hand-delivered my CDs to every radio station that let me across their doorstep. I was on a roll—until my world came crashing down.

I was in the Texas Panhandle for a show. I loved booking events in that area because my folks lived closed to the Lubbock area, so they could come see me. This time, my mom had driven down alone. We went on a shopping trip to Dillard's in the mall, then grabbed a dinner of club sandwiches with broccoli cheese soup at Jason's Deli. She wasn't going to stay for the gig because being jostled by a rowdy crowd in a smoky bar until two o'clock in the morning was not really her scene. So we tried to squeeze in as much time together as possible. After dinner, we sat in her car and giggled about some of my crazy adventures on the road. She asked how I was holding up after recently moving from Nashville back to Texas. Then I told her about my latest crush. He was the man who would end up being my husband, although I didn't know it at the time, and I couldn't stop telling Mom how perfect he was. Finally, we hugged, and she left for home.

It was time for me to start hair and makeup before my show. That consisted of balancing a makeup bag in my lap while I tugged at the rearview mirror of my PT Cruiser, which I had lovingly christened Penelope Tawanda. Ol' Penelope was a hand-me-down from Dad after I sold my car, moved out of my house, and quit my job in Nashville to move back home to Texas. Music City was a little too soul-crushing and a little too far from Mama for me to handle. Penelope Tawanda was my rolling home as I traveled from town to town, hawking my CDs and selling T-shirts on any stage that would let me get up and sing a few songs as an opening act for more well-known Texas country artists.

The next morning, I hit the road early. I had a six-hour drive ahead, but I was fueled up on coffee and puppy love. Upon my arrival in Austin, I would be going on one of my first official dates with Bryan Barrett. I was giddy, and I sang with the windows down my entire drive. I was on the final hour of my drive, planning my date outfit in my head, dreaming about the evening ahead of me, when the phone rang.

I will never forget that call. It was Dad. I could hear the fear in his voice, and immediately, I knew something was wrong.

"Charla... Your mom has had a seizure or a stroke or something. She's been airlifted to a hospital in Amarillo. We don't know what's going to happen. But it's bad. Please pray."

It wasn't just bad. It was terrible. My brother booked me a flight into Amarillo from Austin, as no one wanted me driving back up to the Panhandle in tears. When I arrived at the hospital, the rest of my family was already in the waiting room. The looks on their faces confirmed that mom's condition was worse than anyone had let on over the phone.

She had a massive stroke down the middle of her brain. A middle cerebral artery (MCA) stroke affects speech, writing, walking, driving, working, holding a hot pan or curling iron, bathing—everything Mama needed or loved to do. As devastated as I was, I couldn't imagine what was going through her mind. Because while she had lost most of her motor abilities, but she had not lost any cognitive function. She knew exactly what was going on mentally, yet she could no longer communicate or even perform basic tasks.

But my mom is a fighter. My dad received the first glimmer of hope when he was helping her shower in the handicapped-equipped hospital bathroom. He said, "You know you're getting old when someone else has to wash your hiney."

To which mom popped back, in a choppy cadence but with her familiar sense of humor, "Either that, or you just have enough money to pay someone to wash your hiney." That little comment brought my dad so much comfort. He knew the same Gwen was still in there somewhere. But this once tall, vibrant, commanding, inspiring woman was now stuck in a hospital with no clear sign of what the future would look like. Would she be able to teach high school again? Would she be able to walk down the aisle at my wedding one day? Would she be able to rock her grandbabies again?

After a lengthy stay in intensive care, we all knew there would be a long road of therapy ahead at home. Since I was basically a homeless, traveling musician, it made sense for me to put my music endeavors on hold and move home to care for mom full-time so Dad could continue to work. After months of physical, speech, and occupational therapy, she made some progress, but we knew she would never be the same. And although we grieve the loss of her abilities, we are so thankful we still have our GiGi (Grandma Gwen) with us today.

The experience was terrifying for me. I realized that I had almost lost her. I regretted not documenting every word we ever shared, every piece of advice she had given me, every life lesson she had taught me. I hadn't even had my own babies yet. Who was going to teach me how to be a wife and mother? I barely knew how to cook and do my own laundry, let alone all those other things!

Fast-forward to the present. As I write these words, Mama is alive and feisty as ever, although limited physically. She saw all four of her kids get married and have babies of our own, making her GiGi to fourteen grandbabies. The older grandkids, who knew her before the stroke, are protective of her. They teach compassion to the younger grandkids since they know it's hard for them to understand why GiGi can't talk very well and uses a wheelchair. I watch as they run ahead to hold the door open for other people with disabilities. Life with GiGi has made them acutely aware of the needs of others around us. It's taught all of us countless lessons of faith and grace.

This experience has also given us a whole new appreciation for our dad. Big Ed bathes her, blow-dries her hair, puts in curlers, helps her get dressed, and puts on her jewelry. He brings her food, drives her to get her nails done, and takes her on road trips to see the grandkids as often as possible. That man is a blessing, and I tear up thinking about their love for each other after fifty-three years (and counting) of marriage.

Life can change in an instant. As I look at my own life now, I can't help but think how my daughter would handle it if something happened to me. She is so young. There are still so many life lessons I want to instill in her little heart and mind. I wish I could hand her a guide on how to navigate this life on earth.

I contemplated giving my daughter a handbook of life lessons. Then I realized those lessons were already written in the Bible and illustrated by powerful women whose voices still ring loud and clear today. The twenty-eight stories in the following pages are timeless, but the applications are unique to each of us. These Bible heroes (along with a couple of villains) reveal how to love, believe, and act like daughters of God. We find inspiration in their bravery and faith. We marvel at their cleverness, perseverance, and success. We learn of their troubles, their loneliness, their longing to be loved.

These are unique individuals in the Bible who happen to be women. They do not fit a nice, neat mold. They do not give us a one-size-fits-all pattern that we must conform to if we want to follow God. They are as different from each other as you could imagine, as different as each of us is today, yet their struggles and triumphs reveal common threads of faith, love, and courage.

Let the collective wisdom and experiences of these legendary women speak to you today. Whether you are a teenager, young adult, wife, mother, foster mom, adoptive mom, spiritual mom, aunt, girlfriend, fiancé, divorcee, widow, godmother, grandmother, great-grandmother, girl boss, stay-at-home mom, entrepreneur, businesswoman, retiree, or any other title I'm might not have thought of, you are first and foremost a daughter of God, and the stories in the Bible are there for your encouragement and inspiration.

In each of these letters, I've included a few personal anecdotes from my music and radio career and business endeavors. Not because my story is better or worse than anyone else's, but because I want to share with my daughter and with you the lessons I've learned along the way in the hope that they will help you live your own story to the fullest.

Yes, I'm a mom, writing letters to my daughter. But these are letters my mother could have written to me, or letters your mother could have written to you, or letters you might one day write to your daughter. I hope they become more than pages in a book. I pray they would be a mother's voice guiding you down the path of life.

Thank you for reading, and may you never lose sight of your infinite value as a woman and a daughter of the King.

Eve

Timeless Contentment

DEAR DAUGHTER,

I LOVE LISTENING TO YOU TALK ABOUT WHAT YOU want to be and do when you grow up. You have so many dreams! I know that God has plans for you far beyond what you could even imagine right now. I hope that you never stop dreaming, and I pray that God would give you the desires of your heart.

Here's the thing about dreams, though. They are exciting and motivating, but they can't bring you the fulfillment you truly long for. Only God can do that. No matter what you accomplish in your life—which is going to be a lot!—and no matter where you go, or who you marry, or how much money you make, or what career path you choose, you'll discover that your greatest joy and peace are found in God. Once you learn to be content in Him, to enjoy Him, and to follow Him, you'll never lack satisfaction.

It took me a while to learn this. When I was a child, I was

HERE'S THE THING ABOUT DREAMS, THOUGH. THEY ARE EXCITING AND MOTIVATING, BUT THEY CAN'T BRING YOU THE FULFILLMENT YOU TRULY LONG FOR. ONLY GOD CAN DO THAT.

determined to become the next country music star. I entered every talent show, joined every community theater group, and competed in every local pageant possible to sharpen my performance skills. I attended a music college where I took vocal lessons, learned how to play bass and guitar, learned to sing harmonies as a backup singer, and performed in a band. Then, I cut my college years short after the head of the local opry in Lubbock, TX, told my dad, "Her voice is too big for this small stage. She needs to go to Nashville."

So off I went. I left behind everything I knew and moved four states away to pursue a dream. A dream I was destined for yet entirely unprepared to achieve.

I had never been in the presence of so much incredible talent. Every girl I met in Nashville was more beautiful and more talented than I was. They could write better songs, play their guitar more skillfully, and wear jeans at least two sizes smaller than mine.

I fell into the comparison trap and completely forgot why I had moved to Nashville in the first place. I began to change my hair and makeup. I hired two different performance coaches and a vocal coach. I began to diet and obsess about my physical appearance like never before. I tried so hard to be like the other girls at the writers' rounds that I lost myself. I forgot God had made me perfect in His image. I forgot He had given me unique skills and talents that no one else possessed. I was trying to change everything about myself to fit into a specific box that I thought would help me break into stardom.

I was determined to become the next LeAnn Rimes. She was my music idol, my career goal, my image of success. I remember purchasing her *All That* album at Norman Petty Studios in Clovis, New Mexico when I was eleven years old. I couldn't believe someone my age had cut a record. From that moment, I held onto the notion that if she could do this, I could, too! A seed of stardom was planted that day, and I became laser-focused. I would have given up everything. There was no sacrifice I wasn't willing to make.

Yet, the reality is that my dream was exactly that: *mine*. My will, my plan, and my agenda, not the plan God had for life. I thought my dream was going to be a ticket to happiness and success. I felt I needed the applause of others to validate my worth. But it was always just out of reach, and my overwhelming desire to achieve it threatened to destroy not only my self-esteem, but also my choices, my relationships, and my career.

My misguided devotion to a selfish pursuit reminds me of the story of Eve in Genesis 1. Eve isn't just the first woman mentioned in the Bible, she was the first woman to exist at all. She was created by God, as was Adam, and given free access to the Garden of Eden, a literal paradise on Earth. Yet that wasn't enough for her. She lost her contentment.

Have you ever noticed how easy it is to focus on what we don't have instead of turning our focus on all that we do have? Eve had everything—except the fruit from one tree. There was just one thing that God had said she could not have. And that, of course, was what she wanted.

Eve is an example of what happens when we go after the one thing we can't have—it starts a ripple effect of destruction. Eve was in a good place, after all, a very good place. God had created her and formed her in His image. He had placed her in the most luscious, beautiful paradise called Eden. Every need was met. She ruled and worked together with Adam in the garden. Most importantly, Eve knew God. She knew the sound of His voice and the cadence of His footsteps. Her relationship with her Creator was pure, whole, and healthy. She had complete security.

The devil did not want God to get the glory for all He had created, so he slithered his way into the mind of Eve, making her question what she knew. He fed her thoughts with half-truths and untruths, and he deceived her into justifying lies. He told Eve, "For God knows that when you eat from [the tree of life] your eyes will be opened, and you will be like God, knowing good and evil" (Genesis 3:4 NKJV).

Eve fell for it. She wanted the knowledge, power, and status the devil dangled in front of her. She must have believed taking the fruit would bring her greater happiness. Instead, in an instant, she went from enjoying continual fellowship with God to suffering fear and guilt. From being clothed in freedom to covering her shame with fig leaves. From being one with her Father to making excuses for disobeying Him. From Eden to exile.

Can you imagine everything being right in your world, and suddenly it's not? Maybe there is a knock at your door, and the person standing there carries devastating news, or a phone call brings your world crashing down. I remember one particular time, in the middle of my morning show. I was laughing and cutting up with the others on the program. Everything was fun and carefree. Then my husband called. He never called me while I was on the air. His voice was almost incoherent as he told me his best friend had been murdered. I went from complete happiness to being unable to stand and blinded by tears. I was a puddle on the floor.

That is how I imagine the instant, deafening sorrow that rang across the Garden of Eden when Eve fell victim to the enemy who came to steal, kill, and destroy. Everything changed, all because Eve insisted on pursuing the one thing she couldn't have. She allowed the fruit to consume her heart, her vision, her desire.

Do you know what the good news is, though? God found Adam and Eve. God could have left them in their sin, but instead, He came looking for them. He dealt with their sin and their shame. There were consequences, but there was also mercy. God promised that one day the devil would be defeated. He was talking about Jesus, of course, although they didn't know it at the time.

Daughter, you will face the same dilemma as all daughters of God have. Will you believe the father of lies, or will you believe the Father of Truth? Will you desperately strive for more, comparing yourself to others and assuming you'd be happier if you had what they have, or will you discover the joy and peace of contentment? You are strong and driven, and I love that about you; today, I pray you would learn to wrap that strength and desire in godly contentment.

We often get so consumed with what we don't have that we get disillusioned with what we do have. We think we have a better plan than God. We start to believe our will is better than His, and we move outside of His will. We lose sight of the reality that God has the perfect plan for our lives already written. That is where the hidden power of contentment is found: in our discovery that we already have what we need because we have God.

THAT IS WHERE THE HIDDEN POWER OF CONTENTMENT IS FOUND: IN OUR DISCOVERY THAT WE ALREADY HAVE WHAT WE NEED BECAUSE WE HAVE GOD.

One of my favorite devotional authors, Lysa TerKeurst, compares our hearts to cups. She says that as women, when we feel like we lack in certain areas in our lives, we often look outward for others to fill our cups. We hold our hearts out to the world and ask, "Can you make me feel beautiful? Can you make me feel important?" When we find that other people can't fill those cups, we might turn to food or alcohol or drugs, seeking satisfaction. Or maybe we throw ourselves into work, hobbies, and other activities. We long for our hearts to be full. We think, *If only I had what they have, then I'd be happy. If only I had the job she has, then I'd feel significant.*

This is the danger Eve fell into when she tried to fill her heart with the empty promises of a piece of fruit, and it's the danger we can all so easily fall victim to by holding the cups of our hearts out to the world. We think the world can fill us up better than God can.

In Nashville, I was trying to fill my heart by finding recognition and success within the music world. But I could never find what I so desperately wanted there. I'm convinced that no matter how much success I might have had, it would never have been enough. I needed to find contentment and security in God before I could find peace in my life and career.

I had started to believe the lies that I was unworthy, unwanted, and untalented. It wasn't until I moved back to my home state of Texas several years later that I began to feel comfortable in my own skin. I was so desperate to rediscover the old Charla after I exhausted all my earthly efforts that I finally turned everything about me over to God, and He gave me favor in place of failure. After I left Nashville behind, I found a place where my strengths were celebrated within the Texas music community. My hard work and grit were praised, and in turn, I earned my place at the proverbial table alongside fellow musicians who respected me and saw my worth.

I don't think they would have been as welcoming had I not found my value in Christ Jesus. Once I sought only His approval and stopped seeking outside validation, other people's opinions of me didn't hold much weight. I didn't long to have what LeAnn Rimes or anyone else had; I only wanted to utilize my God-given talents as a way of honoring my Heavenly Father.

Like Eve, we face temptations. And like Eve, we have a Messiah. Jesus helps us overcome the lies and temptations of the enemy. We read in the Gospels about Jesus being tempted by the devil. Jesus felt the same pangs of hunger while His seducer bargained with Him, arguing that he could fill Jesus' earthly cup with all that He desired. Jesus rebuked the temptation in Matthew 4:4, declaring, "It is written, 'Man shall not live by bread alone, but by every word that proceeds from the mouth of God'" (NKJV).

Notice how Jesus immediately took His focus off the temptation and placed it on the will of God. He looked away from the lies and toward His God and Father. We've all heard that saying, "Not today, Satan." That comes from this passage, when Jesus finally says, "Away with you, Satan! For it is written, 'You shall worship the Lord your God, and Him only you shall serve'" (verse 10).

If you turn away from empty pursuits and vain ambitions and turn toward Heaven, God will be there, waiting to fill your cups. Like Eve, you are God's daughter. And like Eve, God pursues you. He always has, always does, always will. God covers your shame. He defeats your enemy. He gives you a place to belong.

If I'm honest, I still struggle at times with my desire to be noticed, to have my needs met, and to feel like I'm respected by my peers. I think some of that could be healthy—it comes from having a passionate, driven spirit and wanting to soak up every moment I have here on Earth. But when I feel my ego creeping in and rearing its ugly head, I know it's time to focus

LIKE EVE, YOU ARE GOD'S DAUGHTER. AND LIKE EVE, GOD PURSUES YOU.

on all that I do have instead of obsessing over all I lack. I pause to keep myself in check. I stop to feed my soul and deny my ego. I lean into God's goodness by fully trusting Him in all situations. I let go of trying to control every aspect of life, and I relinquish authority to the Lord because I learned long ago that control is an illusion.

It's amazing what happens when you don't care what anyone else thinks except God. He is the source of all fulfillment, all validation, all satisfaction. When you choose to follow His plan in gratitude and humility, knowing that He cares for you, life becomes full. You might not achieve some of your childhood dreams, and you'll accomplish other things that you never dreamed of at all. But neither your failures nor successes will alter the peace you've found in God. You'll look around and say, "Life is good, and I am content."

Love,

Mom

Sarah

Timeless Service

DEAR DAUGHTER,

I LOVE HOW STRONG YOU ARE, and yet how kind. You do both of those things so well.

Why do we separate strength and kindness in our heads? Why do we think women should be sweet and kind, but not loud and strong? Or we believe that if they are strong, they cannot also be kind? Maybe it's because we often imagine that *kind* means docile, passive, a pushover; and we imagine that *strong* means overpowering, abrasive, rude.

I think we need to redefine those words. I think we should be both strong and kind at the same time. Just like you.

I try to be sweet and kind, but I'm not naturally a quiet person, as you are well aware. When people refer to me behind my back, I doubt they use words like meek or submissive. I'm pretty sure they would say stubborn-headed and loud. I'm okay with that. My goal isn't to fit someone else's expectation, after all, but to fit God's expectation.

I've always been a strong person. The problem is, when I was younger, I didn't know how to handle my passions, my urges, my pent-up energy. I still cringe at the memories of multiple road trips in my childhood when my dad would slam on the brakes, sending us four kids flying to the front of our sixteen-passenger van (because seatbelts were not yet required), so he could discipline each of us for acting crazy.

My strong and, at times, rebellious spirit would not easily be tamed, though. In my teenage years, I would often crawl out of my bedroom window to go on adventures with my girlfriends in the middle of the night. When I would sneak back into my bed, thinking I was as quiet as a mouse, Dad would be sitting in the dark in the corner of my room. After scaring me half to death, he would ground me for my disobedience. Nothing got past him. I think I spent most of my high school years grounded because I couldn't relinquish my rebellious spirit. I didn't know how to give up my need to be in control. I wanted to have the final say in my life. I wanted to do things my way.

I didn't fully let go of my selfish ways until I met your dad. I knew very quickly he was *the one*. He had every one of my favorite qualities. He was perfect. He was handsome and strong. He was also quiet and stoic. He is a man of few words, so when he did speak, people listened. Even on the night we met, I think the only words he said were, "Can I have your number?"

I knew I needed to straighten up my act so I wouldn't

blow it. I had a feeling my loud, boisterous personality might be a little too much for him to handle. So, I quieted my voice. I listened to his cadence. I worked

YOU CAN BE BOTH STRONG AND KIND, BOLD AND TENDER, COURAGEOUS AND HUMBLE WHEN YOU LEARN TO SERVE IN LOVE.

to match his demeanor. I wanted to honor him and follow wherever he led. Somehow, I knew it was time to give in to the work God had been trying to do in my life for the last twenty-eight years. I couldn't be footloose and fancy-free if I wanted to stand by his side as his wife. It was time to become the princess God wanted me to be. It was time to be a handmaiden and not a handful.

Please know that I am not talking about denying who I am. I'm still loud and spontaneous and strong, and that won't ever change. Instead, I'm talking about learning to control myself in order to serve others. About living for loved ones, friends, and people in need, not just for myself. About choosing to use my strength to be kind and loving.

That is my message for you. You can choose to serve. You can be both strong and kind, bold and tender, courageous and humble when you learn to serve in love. Love brings out the best in you.

One of the clearest biblical examples of using strength to serve is seen in the life of Sarah, the wife of Abraham, whose story is recorded in the book of Genesis. Many biblical scholars say Sarah is the most documented woman in the Bible. Her name means "princess," and she was a beautiful woman. Sarah began a family that would eventually grow into a nation. She was the mother of Israel, and she was the mother of our faith.

Sarah's journey toward motherhood was not easy, though. She was barren for many decades. When God finally fulfilled His promise to give her a child, she was a whopping ninety years old. Can you imagine? Sarah had laughed at God's promise when she first received it because she had long since given up hope. But she was able to believe Him despite her advanced age. Hebrews 11:11 tells us, "And by faith even Sarah, who was past childbearing age, was enabled to bear children because she considered him faithful who had made the promise." Talk about strength, tenacity, and spunk! Sarah never gave up on her dreams.

Can you picture her waddling into a room, her ninety-year-old pregnant belly leading the way? There are two questions you should never ask a woman: "Are you pregnant?" and "How old are you?" But I'm sure *everyone* asked Sarah *both* of those questions. She would have been the center of everyone's conversation because, after all those years of waiting, God had granted her the greatest miracle of all.

What impresses me most about Sarah, though, was her ability to follow Abraham with such faithfulness. She was strong, beautiful, and brave, but she was also a servant. Peter writes about the women of old, "They submitted themselves to their own husbands, like Sarah, who obeyed Abraham and called him her lord. You are her daughters if you do what is right and do not give way to fear" (1 Peter 3:6). Sarah could have chosen to use her strength and her beauty for herself, but instead, she understood the value of serving her family and her God. She knew she was called to serve, to love, to give. And as a result, she became the mother of a nation. She was faithful to follow God's will for her, and God was faithful to give her the desires of her heart.

In today's society, the idea of a wife "submitting" to her husband often has a negative connotation. We imagine ourselves cowering under the commanding rule of our husband, granting his every wish. But being submissive is simply having a servant's heart. To serve my husband is to serve the Lord. I love to honor my children, my parents, and my friends by serving them.

Remember that Abraham loved Sarah. He doted over her. They had a great marriage and good communication, and they loved each other very much. The idea of calling him "lord" was not one of abject servitude but of respect. And I'm sure it was mutual respect.

I see this in my marriage, as well. There is no sense of power or control, but rather one of unwavering devotion with respect and admiration for one another. Just like Abraham and Sarah, your dad and I talk about everything. We make plans together. In one sense, he is the spiritual leader in our family whom I fully trust to walk beside on this life journey to unknown lands. But he trusts me as well. He listens to me, and I listen to him, and together we are stronger than either of us would be on our own.

Two verses before the one I quoted above, Peter writes that the most extraordinary beauty of Sarah and other heroes of the Bible was their "inner self, the unfading beauty of a gentle and quiet spirit, which is of great worth in God's sight" (verse 4). Sarah was so beautiful that Abraham was afraid he would be killed by anyone who wanted to have her. The Egyptian Pharaoh even tried to take her as his wife before he knew she was married. Yet, for us today, her greatest fame is her inner beauty, her self-control, her ability to turn her strength toward service.

That phrase "gentle and quiet" is a hard one for me. I'm not going to lie. Again, those are not adjectives people typically use when they think of Charla. I've come to realize, though, that being quiet is the first step toward serving others. Not quiet in the sense of passive or stifled or oppressed, but in the sense of listening to the voice of God and looking for opportunities to be His hands and feet here on Earth. Being gentle and quiet does not mean you are inferior. I believe it puts you at the feet of God, which is the highest place you could be.

In Scripture, "gentle" does not mean weak. It carries the idea of a wild horse who is tamed by a loving master. My old nature was like an untamed, bucking stallion, thrashing around with muscle and power to break free from being constrained. My renewed nature is one of a tamed horse, where the simple pull of the reins by the Holy Spirit will lead me down the path I need to follow. I long to have a servant spirit toward the Lord and do as He asks of me, no matter how simple or difficult. I am strong, but it's strength under control, a strength that God can use to serve people around me.

We all have a wild side of our hearts that wants to be free of boundaries, rules, or guidelines. At times, we want to cast off restraint and to live for ourselves. However, I have learned over the years that I need to ask God to tame the wild side of me that could lead me away from His goodness and all the blessings He wants to work in my life—blessings like marrying your dad!

Is it always easy to choose service and self-control? Of course not. I fight that wild stallion deep in my soul nearly every day. I want to set my to-do list on fire and head for the beach. I look at the dirty dishes in the sink and imagine throwing them out the back window, hoping no one will notice. I think if I smell one more dirty diaper, I might lose my mind. If only I could take a long, uninterrupted bubble bath and zone out while reading a juicy romance novel, I might gain some of my sanity back.

In those moments, I ask the Lord to restore my gentle and quiet spirit. Instead of saying, "I have to do the dishes," I say, "I am so thankful to have food on the table, and I'm glad I get to clean the dishes after a healthy meal." Instead of saying, "I have to do laundry," I say, "Thank you, Lord, for blessing me with clothes on my family's back. I'm thankful to fold and put away my precious children's clothes." Instead of saying, "I have to clean the house again," I say, "I get to honor my family by keeping cleanliness a priority."

Full disclosure: sometimes it takes a while to get there. But I wouldn't trade this life for anything. It is a blessing to serve.

Social media tells us, "You do you, Boo." I think a better phrase would be, "You do Jesus, Boo." Listen to the wisdom of God, refuse to give in to the fears of life, and stand firm in your faith. As you follow Jesus and his love, you'll discover ful-

I AM STRONG, BUT IT'S STRENGTH UNDER CONTROL, A STRENGTH THAT GOD CAN USE TO SERVE PEOPLE AROUND ME.

fillment that living for yourself could never provide.

Having a servant's heart for God will be your greatest joy. I pray God would bring a man who also possesses a servant's heart into your life and that you would be his princess, just as you are God's princess. I pray that you would discover the fulfillment that comes from using your strength and your kindness to serve.

Be strong. Be kind. Be *you.*

Love,

Mom

Rebekah

Timeless Strength

DEAR DAUGHTER,

I LOVE GOING ON WALKS WITH YOU. YOU CHASE butterflies and collect dandelions. You point out budding flowers and birds chirping in the trees. You drink in the smell of honeysuckles and wave up at the plane in the sky. You don't see the sadness in the eyes of the man on the park bench or the hollow gaze of the teenager wandering the path, probably skipping school. You see the best in people rather than pointing out flaws. You see all the light and goodness the world has to offer. Your eyes are not focused on differences but on beauty and curiosity.

I know a time will come when those vibrant colors will be mixed with gray. You'll see not just the beauty but also the pain in life. You'll realize that differences are not always celebrated, that people are not always kind, that life doesn't always come easy.

As you grow, I hope I've equipped you with tools to discover the wonder of God's creation, especially in how beautiful and wonderfully He created *you*. I pray you would celebrate the differences in yourself and in others with grace and kindness. I pray your smile would linger and grow as you always remember that God loves you just as you are.

My dear daughter, you *will* be different. You won't always look or talk or act like the world says you should. You will stand out from the crowd, and that is a beautiful thing.

Can we talk about differences? Most of us are so concerned with fitting in that we don't realize our differences are our greatest strengths.

I learned this the hard way. I used to hate my smile. Not as a young child, but later, when my baby teeth began to fall out and my adult teeth came in. I think it started in seventh grade. That was when a boy told me I had horse teeth. He made an obnoxious neighing sound to emphasize his point. I suddenly became aware that I had an incredibly large grill.

I was mortified. I grew self-conscious and insecure about the immense expanse of gums that would show when I would laugh. I don't think I smiled enough to show my teeth until I was well into college. In all my high school senior photos, I'm grinning, but my mouth is closed tight to avoid revealing my prominent teeth.

Do you ever feel insecure about your body? Maybe about your teeth, like me, or the texture of your hair, or the shade of your skin. Maybe about a body part or a physical trait that seems to stand out. Maybe you were oblivious to those differences until someone brought them to your attention with cruel derision. It wasn't until their words cut you like a knife that you realized you were different.

God doesn't want your differences to make you self-conscious, though. He wants them to be your strength. God made you how you are, and He has a plan for your life—but that plan requires you to be *you*. Different. Strong. Beautiful.

The life of Rebekah, found in Genesis 24, illustrates the strength found in our differences. To understand her story, we must begin with Abraham, who, as you may know, became a father much later in life than most people do—when he was one hundred years old!

Abraham's son was named Isaac. When Isaac grew up, Abraham knew he had to find a wife for him. In those days, you didn't meet your husband in college, at a bar, in church, or on a dating app. Families would arrange the union of a bride and groom, and some marriages were decided as early as birth.

GOD DOESN'T WANT YOUR DIFFERENCES TO MAKE YOU SELF-CONSCIOUS, THOUGH. HE WANTS THEM TO BE YOUR STRENGTH.

Abraham requested that his servant set out on a long journey to find a wife. The servant took ten camels on this mission. When he reached the town where he would find a wife for Isaac, he stopped to get a drink of water. The servant prayed to the God of Abraham to send him a woman who would be willing not only to give him a drink of water, but who would also offer to provide water for his ten camels. Surely such a bold, selfless act would be a sign that this woman was the perfect companion for Isaac.

He saw Rebekah coming with water from the spring, and he asked her for a drink. She set down the jar and gave him water to drink. When he had finished, Rebekah offered, "I'll draw water for your camels, too, until they have finished drinking." She quickly emptied her jar into the trough and ran back to the spring to get more water.

To understand this story fully, you have to realize that one gallon of water weighs eight pounds. A thirsty camel can drink up to thirty gallons of water. Remember, there were ten camels. That means Rebekah had to run back and forth from the spring to supply 300 gallons of water. That's a total of 2,400 pounds. We're talking about as much weight as a small car.

I imagine Rebekah with broad shoulders and large biceps, like a WWE wrestler. Think of the hours she must have spent at the local CrossFit gym, shoulder-pressing baby goats, doing snatch-and-cleans with donkeys, and dominating at yoke walks. I bet some bully in her middle-school science class made a comment or two about the girth of her biceps. Rebekah was one fierce chick. But it wasn't just her physical strength and stamina that stand out in her story. She was strong in her mind, will, and emotions as well, as we learn from what happened next.

After this encounter, which likely took around three hours, the servant showered Rebekah with fine jewelry as gifts from Abraham. He requested to speak with her family so he could ask for their consent to take Rebekah as Isaac's wife. Her family was willing to give her hand in marriage to Isaac, but they were hesitant to say goodbye to her so quickly, so they asked for more time to decide and say their farewells.

The servant said his mission was urgent, that Abraham had waited long enough, and that he needed a decision immediately.

Rebekah, strong and bold, jumped in. "I will go now." She left her family and all she had ever known up to that point in her life. She took only her nurse, a single familiar face, on the long journey to meet her future husband.

Talk about a strong woman! Not just physical strength to carry all that water to feed his camels, but mental and emotional strength to accept the servant's proposal, to say goodbye to her family, to bravely face the unknown. Like so many other women of the Bible, she was powerful, resilient, and smart. She was eager in spirit and willing to give of herself, which placed her perfectly into God's plan for His people. Her tenacity and courage made her different, and her differences were key to her success.

Can you imagine being in her position? Do you think you would have had the courage to pick up and leave your family with so little time to contemplate if it were the right decision or not? I know you would have. I know that you, like Rebekah, are strong, that you speak for yourself, that you embrace the future with confidence in God and in yourself.

When Rebekah arrived at Abraham and Isaac's home, Isaac fell in love with her. We read, "Then Isaac brought her into his mother Sarah's tent; and he took Rebekah and she became his wife, and he loved her. So Isaac was comforted after his mother's death" (Genesis 24:67 NKJV). Together, Rebekah and Isaac carried on God's plan to raise up His chosen nation of Israel. Many centuries later, the Messiah, Jesus himself, was born from their descendants,

There is more to Rebekah's story, of course. She didn't have an easy life. She dealt with twenty years of barrenness, some crazy family conflict, and more. But through it all, her story is one of unstoppable strength, of courage to embrace opportunities, of a willingness to write her own future. No, she didn't fit all the expectations of what a woman and wife should be in that culture—submissive, quiet, vulnerable—and that was a good thing. It was part of God's plan to turn a family into a nation and ultimately to bring salvation to the world.

It took me a long time—and the assistance of braces and retainers—to grow into my smile. But my emotional misalignment was harder to fix than my overbite. I had to come to terms with the fact that God did not create me with this big, gummy smile just for me to hide it or be ashamed of it. Instead, He wanted me to become a woman who was unapologetic about how perfectly and wonderfully He had made me.

Ironically, the discomfort of feeling different motivated

me to find ways to turn my difference into strength. Because I was so self-conscious about my teeth, I became quick with my tongue. I took speech and acting classes in college. I forced myself to enter every talent show and to book speaking engagements in front of as many people as I possibly could. I honed my skill of the gift of gab. I learned to score parts and land jobs.

One note: those same skills got me into trouble a few times. As quickly as my words can build someone up, they can cut someone down if I'm not careful. While I tend to think I'm helping a situation by intervening and voicing my opinion, I've had to force myself to do more listening than talking. God gave us two ears and one mouth for a reason, right? On more than a few occasions, I've regretted letting out words that should have remained caged behind these horse teeth. Remember that your strength can also be a weakness if you don't act with wisdom, love, and humility.

Those mistakes aside, though, I have nothing but gratitude now for my big mouth. If my smile were "normal," I might never have landed some of the roles I was honored to fill in my music and radio career. It takes a big mouth to be on a morning show for five years! And what about the people I reached by yapping my giant gums on stage in front of an audience? I might not have caught their attention without my loud mouth.

One of the greatest compliments I've ever received came from an acting coach in college. He told me I had the best smile because it was infectious and lit up the entire room, lifting the spirits of everyone around me. "You bring the sunshine," he said.

Our differences are our gift to the world around us. The things we think are holding us back are often the exact things God will use to reach and serve people. What we might view as a curse actually propels us into our purpose.

Over time, I found peace and clarity about why God had given me certain gifts to offer this world. As I spent time knowing God and listening to him, I realized He made me this way, He loves me this way, and He uses me this way. Not a single one of my gifts was for my glory, but rather to be used to point all the glory to Him and to serve the people He loves so much.

Today, I adore my big, gummy smile. I just wish it hadn't taken me so many years to truly appreciate God's gifts.

How about you? What makes you feel self-conscious and different? What do you wish you could change about yourself? Maybe you wish your hair were straighter or curlier, but it always seems to be somewhere in the middle. Or maybe you have a healthy appetite for life, but you find yourself comparing your body to all the girls you double-tap to like while scrolling

HE MADE ME THIS WAY, HE LOVES ME THIS WAY, AND HE USES ME THIS WAY.

social media. Maybe you think you are too loud, or too quiet, or too driven, or too merciful. Whatever it is, God is saying, "If only you would spend as much time with Me as you do obsessing over your insecurity, I could free you. You're going to love who

I created you to be. Just trust Me."

I pray you would love yourself as God loves you. He knows every hair on your head. He understands every little detail of your heart. He longs for you to be exactly who He made you to be.

The only way to truly find yourself and accept every part of who you are is by getting to know the God who built you. So, stop scrolling through Instagram, and start flipping through the Bible. You'll find you are exactly who you are supposed to be when you know who you are in Christ.

Different. Strong. Beautiful.

Love,

Mom

Leah

Timeless Praise

DEAR DAUGHTER,

I LOVE GOING TO THE MOVIES WITH YOU. We kick back with our popcorn in hand and sneak the chocolate bars I have stashed in my purse while sipping on a bubbly soda that tickles our noses. We love escaping our own lives and being transported into the middle of someone else's story. We drink in their adventure, their struggle, and at the end, their happily-ever-after love or triumph.

But can you imagine if we went to a movie that never resolved after those two hours of cinematic imagery? What if the guy never got the girl, the treasure was never discovered, the bad guy was never defeated, or the lost dog was never found? What if the story just kept going, without end, no matter how long we sat there and watched the movie? What if there were sad parts that didn't make sense, tragedies that made us cry, hard choices that didn't have an easy solution? What if there were hours of boring parts where people just kept doing what they had to do, living and loving and being faithful?

That doesn't sound like a movie. It sounds more like normal life.

Life doesn't always make sense. It has good parts and bad parts and boring parts and exciting parts. It's not always fair, and justice is not always done. Sometimes there is pain that we can't explain or can't change.

A precious friend of mine does humanitarian work to advocate for women who have been exploited or trafficked or who are domestic violence victims. The stories she has shared with me break my heart: the loss of innocence and all the things taken from them and done to them, often at such young ages. I cry over the injustice and pain of their stories. I turn to God in prayer, and then do what I can to fight injustice around me. That is why my friend works so hard: she wants to do everything she possibly can to bring aid and safety to those who are suffering.

There are some parts of life we can't understand. Only Heaven will bring true peace, justice, and rest. I don't say that to excuse inaction now—we must do what we can. But we also have to find peace even when things don't make sense. We have to see the blessings God has given us even when the story doesn't resolve, the good guys don't seem to be winning, and there are more questions than answers.

Here's what I've found: the blessings of God are not always found at the end, when the story resolves, but rather within the struggles themselves. God is faithful even when things don't make sense. He gives us inner peace even when we are going through storms. His blessings are not just the gifts He gives, but His constant presence and love.

It is this presence of God that enables us to praise Him always—no matter what happens, or where we find ourselves, or whether our dreams are coming true, or if people around us are validating us or not. Praise is not just something we do or say, but a lifestyle and attitude of trust that sustains us when we haven't seen the final answer.

THE BLESSINGS OF GOD ARE NOT ALWAYS FOUND AT THE END, WHEN THE STORY RESOLVES, BUT RATHER WITHIN THE STRUGGLES THEMSELVES.

As I read the stories of women in the Bible, I see example after example of women who were able to praise God even when the circumstances they were living were far from ideal. They discovered blessings that went beyond happy endings and cheesy Disney plotlines. They met God, and God Himself became the reason for their joy.

The story of Leah in Genesis 29 is an illustration of praise and blessings in the midst of struggle. Leah's life was far from a fairy tale. To make a long story short, Isaac and Rebekah's son Jacob fell in love with a woman named Rachel. Rachel's father, Laban, promised Jacob that if he worked for him for seven years, he would let Jacob marry her.

How could Laban make him work seven years just to earn the hand of Rachel? At the time, Jacob was a fugitive. He and his mother Rebekah had stolen his brother's birthright, after all. Now he was on the run with only the shirt on his back and nothing to offer in exchange for a bride. Laban knew this, and he took advantage of Jacob, who would do anything for Rachel because he was madly in love with her.

Sounds like a movie, right? Only it didn't work out how you would expect. Jacob worked for seven years. At the end of that time, Laban took advantage of him again, in the cruelest way possible. On the wedding night, Laban deceived Jacob by giving him Rachel's older sister Leah as his bride instead. Leah would have been hidden behind a veil, and Jacob didn't realize he had been tricked until the next morning when he awoke.

Can you imagine how hurt Leah must have been when she saw the disappointment in Jacob's eyes? Jacob yelled at Laban, "What is this you have done to me? I served you for Rachel" (verse 25). That must have wounded Leah's heart so deeply.

Laban concocted another manipulative bargain to squeeze more years of labor out of Jacob. He told him to wait through the week of wedding festivities, and then he would give him Rachel as a second wife—if Jacob agreed to work another seven years. So that's what happened. Jacob took both sisters as his wives, and he worked for Laban for another seven years.

Keep in mind, marrying more than one wife was not ordained by God. From the beginning, He said marriage would be between one man and one woman. Having multiple wives was a pagan practice. Having multiple wives who were *sisters*, though, is another level of weird and wrong altogether.

There is very little that is good about this story. Jacob was forced to work for fourteen years. Rachel was forced to become a second wife, after her sister, rather than sharing the love story she had imagined with the husband of her dreams. But the person who got the worst end of the deal was Leah. She didn't have a say in any of her circumstances. Her father used her as a bargaining tool. Jacob never chose her, and her younger, more beautiful sister resented her. Leah became the unloved wife, the mistake, the reject. As we look at her story, we should feel compassion for her unwarranted situation. Who was on Leah's side in any of this?

Understandably, Leah longed for love. But she didn't receive it. The Bible says that Jacob loved Rachal but not Leah.

Here's what we can learn, though. The devastating rejection Leah faced also stirred her to fight, grow, pray, and learn. She found blessings even in pain. That doesn't excuse the tragedy and abuse against her—but it does remind us that God is bigger than our circumstances, and He is faithful even when those around us fail us. Like Leah, our blessings can come through our pain.

God didn't abandon Leah. The author of Genesis says this: "When the Lord saw that Leah was unloved, He opened her womb; but Rachel was barren" (29:31 NKJV).

Did you catch that? The Lord *saw* her. Leah must have realized that God knew of her struggles the entire time. He had always been there. Somehow, this was all going to work together for good.

Leah was seen by God Himself. Rachel was still barren at this point, but God blessed Leah with four sons in a row. In the culture of the day, this solidified her position with Jacob by fulfilling her goal as a wife of providing male heirs. It was a sign of God's blessing and care, even though she must have suffered greatly in her marriage.

Leah longed for love, and she thought she could find that in Jacob. After the birth of each of her first three sons, Reuben, Simeon, and Levi, she stated that *now* Jacob would surely love her because she had given him sons. After her fourth son, though, she said something different. She changed her perspective. She stopped seeking validation by Jacob and instead focused on God. The transformation in her heart was evident when she said simply, "Now I will praise the Lord!" (verse 35). She even named her fourth son Judah, which means praise. In other words, she knew God loved her, and that was what mattered most.

EVEN WHEN OTHERS DON'T RECOGNIZE YOUR TRUE VALUE, GOD DOES.

While we never discover if Leah found favor with Jacob, we know she found favor in the eyes of her Heavenly Father. At the end of her story, Leah was buried next to Jacob in the Promised

Land, where Abraham, Sarah, Isaac, and Rebekah were buried. (Rachel was not buried there because she had died while they were traveling.) To me, it seems like even in death, God was making sure Leah was remembered and honored.

Is it wrong to long for an earthly love story? Of course not. But we don't find our validation in the love of a spouse. Can you imagine the years of heartache Leah could have saved herself if she would have sought a relationship with the Lord sooner rather than seeking validation from an earthly man?

Don't depend on people around you to tell you how much you're worth. Look to God for that. Other people can celebrate you, they can offer their thoughts, they can share their opinions—but nobody truly sees your whole heart like God does. Read the Bible and seek a relationship with Him to discover who you are and *whose* you are in Christ Jesus. Even when others don't recognize your true value, God does. God sees you. He knows you. He made you for His purpose. If other people don't see it, that's on them. It doesn't change you. Don't minimize who you are to make insecure people feel better about themselves. If your dreams are too big for some people, it may be time to say, "Bye Felicia," and put up some healthy boundaries.

I love how Leah said, "Now I will praise." Always have a *now* praise. That means praise that springs from choice, not just from feelings or circumstances. My prayer for your life is that you would have a firm foundation built upon praise because you know who God is, no matter what; that your praise would not be contingent on what is happening around you, but instead would spring from the knowledge that God is working everything together for good.

Her words make me think of Psalm 34:1, "I will bless the Lord at all times" (NKJV). This verse doesn't say most of the time, or 80% of the time, or when I get around to it or feel like I'm in the right mood. It says, "at all times." Do you know who wrote that verse? King David, a direct descendent of Leah and Jacob. I can imagine Leah repeating those words to her children until they became a mantra passed on for generations. They are a reminder that God sees you. Praise Him in your struggles. Praise Him in your darkness. Praise Him now, not just at the finish line. When you have no words to pray, *praise*. I've learned the answer to so many of life's problems comes from praising, even when I don't feel like it. Remember, we may not see a finish line on this side of Heaven—but God's validation is enough.

I remember a season of our lives when we were going through a never-ending

domino effect of challenges, and we didn't think we could handle one more test of will. We had recently moved into a different house, you had switched schools, your dad was getting his construction business off the ground, and the world was going through a global pandemic. In the middle of that, I received a text message. A foster baby needed a loving home. Except the agency wasn't looking for a temporary home for her. They were looking for a forever home.

At that moment, I should have felt overwhelmed with gratitude, I know. But to be honest, I was just overwhelmed. Our world was spinning off its axis. What should have been the biggest blessing for our family felt more like a heavy weight. It was all too much to handle. How were we going to add one more innocent child into our already chaotic mess?

What did we do? We praised. We praised by lifting our hands and voices in song. We praised with prayer and fasting. We praised by reading our Bible and getting into the Word. We praised by sharing our story and our faith with other people. We praised God for the many blessings He had bestowed on us. We praised by getting on our knees to cry out, "Jesus! If we're supposed to say yes to this baby in this unlikely season, we will answer your call."

We did answer that call. And it wasn't always easy. But every day, even in the toughest situations, we praised. We praised before, during, and after the adoption of our precious baby girl. We praise God today for His perfect timing in completing our family. Now, we couldn't imagine life without your baby sister being in the middle of our crazy, wonderful, jumbled-up, fantastical mess of a family.

God never makes mistakes. Even when His plan may not seem like it makes sense, redemption will come. It shows up when you least expect it, in ways you never imagined, through circumstances that are often blessings in disguise. God brings peace that goes beyond logic or understanding. And our response is praise.

As you grow older and wiser, I hope you always see the window of opportunity to praise in the midst of all your circumstances, good or bad. I pray you would learn to walk in the same timeless peace that Leah found in the Lord. Maybe you'll see the answers to your prayers in this life, or maybe your redemption is awaiting you in Heaven. Regardless, just like Leah's story, know that God is always reaching down to you from Heaven, saying, "I see you. I know you. I love you."

Love,

Mom

Puah & Shiphrah

Timeless Courage

DEAR DAUGHTER,

I KNOW THAT SOMETIMES YOU FEEL SCARED. When you do, I am there for you, helping you find courage and peace. One time I had to convince you and your brother that the noise outside your window was just the wind, not a witch on a broomstick.

Did you know that I often feel afraid, too? I think we all do, no matter how young or old we are. I've learned something important about fear, though: *fear is a liar*. This is a motto I live by and something I often say. It's written in various notepads strewn around my desk and nightstand. You'll find it inscribed on wall hangings around our home. I say it to my team in business when they sense fear creeping in, trying to rob them of their dreams.

Fear is a liar; however, the human emotions that come with fear are genuine. That is, our feelings are real, but what they are telling us is often untrue. That is why we must constantly remind ourselves that we don't have to believe what fear says.

Paul wrote in 2 Timothy 1:7, "For God has not given us a spirit of fear, but of power and of love and of a sound mind" (NKJV). Here's where my inquisitive mind starts to churn, though. If we're not supposed to hold onto fear, why are we instructed in other passages to fear the Lord? We need to understand the difference between fearing the Lord and having a spirit of fear.

The Bible tells us the fear of the Lord is the beginning of wisdom. This fear is not a terror or phobia. The Hebrew meaning of fear is to respect or to hold in the highest reverence. This fear doesn't lead to cowering and drawing away, but rather, it propels us to draw near to living in the deep and holy trust of God.

WE MUST CONSTANTLY REMIND OURSELVES THAT WE DON'T HAVE TO BELIEVE WHAT FEAR SAYS.

A" spirit of fear," on the other hand, is the opposite of trusting God. This kind of fear comes from the devil, the enemy of our souls, and it seeks to destroy us, to paralyze us, to steal from us.

Believe me, I know what the wrong kind of fear feels like because it almost derailed my career. It didn't start that way, though. Fear crept in when I was least expecting it.

See, I practically grew up on stage. From a very young age, I was consistently putting myself in uncomfortable situations. I actually enjoyed controlling my nerves. It was a chess game of sorts, where I would take charge of those butterflies in my stomach before they had the chance to turn into anxiety. At family reunions, I would pull out all the stops, dress up in a full get-up of wigs and costumes, and perform crazy routines for my family. Often, my brother would play the piano as I sang church hymns or Christmas carols. I sang at weddings, funerals, school talent shows, and local opries. I competed in every pageant I could enter. If there was a stage to perform on, I found it.

Internal fears and nerves didn't exist early on. I don't even remember feeling nervous when I was little. It was as if I had stepped on stage so often that I had figured out how to short-circuit my nerves. My urge to perform was born from simply wanting to get a smile or a chuckle out of my family. However, as I grew older, I began to perform for the admiration of others, and I connected that admiration to my own worth and potential. Their opinion of me carried weight, which impacted my self-image and my view of my own abilities. That is what opened the door to fear.

Fear took on a life of its own when I started attending South Plains College in Levelland, Texas. I had landed a scholarship there to hone my music skills in their commercial arts program. South Plains College has birthed stars such as Le-Anne Womack, Natalie Maines of the Dixie Chicks, and countless others. It's also where my older brother attended. I'm his biggest fan, and I've followed him around like a puppy dog most of my life.

There I was, possessing complete confidence in my talent as a young performer. But I let fear come in, and the devil saw his opening. I should have expected the "real world" to be a little bit cruel, but I wasn't prepared. I got a good dose of reality and a swift slap to the face regarding my abilities. Family and friends had told me my whole life, "You're such a good singer" and "You're so talented." Suddenly I was hearing, "There are a lot of things you need to work on, including your stage presence and pitch." They would tell me, "If you want to survive in the music industry, you need to be a triple threat. That means singing, songwriting, and playing instruments."

I wasn't equipped to navigate constructive criticism my first year out from under my parents' roof. The devil knew this, and he pounced. I went from never having a fearful bone in my body to being completely consumed with a spirit of fear.

That's exactly what fear is: a spirit placed in your soul by the devil. His goal is to take your greatest gifts and use them against you. There I was, born to sing and perform with the gifts God had given me, but all of a sudden, I was so overcome with nerves that I would even lose my voice before stepping on stage at times. My will and my body were breaking down until I couldn't function under the fear.

The Bible gives us plenty of examples of women who faced far greater threats and fears than stage fright, of course. When I imagine examples of courage, I often think of Puah and Shiphrah, two midwives who cared for the Israelite mothers and infants during childbirth when Israel was enslaved in Egypt. You can read the story in Exodus 1. The Pharaoh, the powerful ruler of Egypt, was afraid that Israel would grow too strong for the Egyptians to control. He commanded Puah and Shiphrah to kill all the male Hebrew babies that were born. We read that "The midwives, however, feared God and did not do what the king of Egypt had told them to do; they let the boys live" (verse 17).

Notice that phrase, "feared God." Even though their very lives were threatened, these two women refused to give in to fear. Why? Because they feared God more.

Fear of Pharaoh led only to abuse and death. But the midwives' fear of God led them to courageous obedience and love. They used their quick thinking and cleverness to outsmart the king. They told him the Hebrew women were stronger and more vigorous than the Egyptian women, giving birth before a midwife could get to them. They were savvy women, willing to risk their own lives to save the children. Puah and Shiphrah remind us that the king's evilness was no match for the goodness of God. Their refusal to give into Pharaoh earned them favor in the eyes of God for their faithfulness.

The story goes on to say, "So God was kind to the midwives and the people increased and became even more numerous. And because the midwives feared God, he gave them families of their own" (verses 20-21).

WE HAVE NOTHING TO BE AFRAID OF IF WE FEAR GOD.

The midwives' heroic actions ultimately allowed the birth of an infant named Moses. God later used Moses to guide the Israelite people out of slavery. It is a beautiful story reminding us that we have nothing to be afraid of if we fear God. When the devil instills in us a spirit of fear, we conquer him through the fear of the Lord.

Now, back to my struggle. This idea of conquering the spirit of fear with the fear of the Lord didn't take root in my heart until I was well into my thirties. I vividly remember overwhelming feelings of uneasiness before performing the national anthem for a Nascar race at Texas Motor Speedway. I usually wouldn't have let my nerves get so out of control, but this time, my performance was to be broadcast on national television in front of an audience of millions of viewers. The spirit of fear began to swirl in my head. What if I fall on the stairs when I take the stage? What if I faint during the pastor's prayer right before I'm supposed to sing? What if I start on the wrong note and the key becomes too high for me to hit during the song's peak? What if the echoes from the stands throw my timing way off because of the delay? What if my blouse pops open and everyone sees my bra on national television? Oh my gosh, what if there's a booger on my face?

But it was too late to reach up and check for any slime hanging from my nose. The cameras flashed on, and the crew pointed that it was my cue.

"Oh, say, can you see..."

But I couldn't see anything. The atmosphere around me faded away. Everything was a blur of sound and nerves.

After one minute and seventeen seconds, my moment was over. I actually did it. I pulled it off, and nothing terrible happened. I didn't die. The world didn't end.

It wasn't my greatest vocal performance because my nerves managed to rear their ugly head just in the back of my throat, but I still managed to more or less nail it. I remember sitting alone in my trailer after it was all said and done, kicking myself for getting so worked up. It had been a thrilling experience, and I sat there, wishing I could go back and relive it without all the nervous energy.

That was when it hit me. The devil had almost won by instilling a spirit of fear in me, but I serve a God who is greater than a spirit of fear and evil. Too bad I didn't have that moment of enlightenment *before* stepping on the stage instead of after!

After that, I began to use the fear of God to combat those emotions that would creep up before any big performance. I would go into this dance of internal dialog and deep breathing, reminding myself that I was using my God-given talents to serve Him. Not using those talents would be doing Him a disservice and would surely dishonor God. I would allow the fear of letting my God-given talents go to waste rise above the emotions of every other fear. I would proclaim a spirit of fear was not welcome on any stage I set foot on. Sure, I could use the feelings of excitement to propel me into a greater performance, but paralyzing fear had no place. I would breathe in God's faithfulness and breathe out courage.

Over the years, I've performed in countless venues. I went from singing in small-town theaters to taking on much bigger stages. I opened shows for top-selling country artists like Asleep at the Wheel and Willie Nelson. I played in front of crowds of fifteen thousand fans. I performed the "Star-Spangled Banner" before professional sporting events. I was in front of the camera on CMT (Country Music Television) and behind the microphone on a top-rated morning radio show. I've spoken in front of hundreds of entrepreneurs and field professionals. I virtually trained thousands of eager business owners. I've led worship and spoken in church.

Each time, those seeds of fear try to take root in the depths of my gut. They still do. But I know how to find courage by drawing close to God.

To be honest, the devil tried to tell me I wasn't qualified to write this book. However, I knew God had placed it on my heart for a divine purpose—to reach people with His truth. I cared more about what God might do if I *didn't* answer His calling than I did about potential rejection from nay-sayers. Reminding myself of God's calling and presence filled me with courage. It gave me the strength to obey His purpose.

You may not be stepping on a stage to perform in front of an audience or congregation, but fear will always challenge you when you try to walk into your destiny, whatever that might look like one day. If you are not seated confidently in your identity in Christ, the devil may see an opening and try to take you down using fear as his weapon of choice. Do not let him! Remember, fear is a big, fat liar.

Think about the deepest desire of your heart or your greatest dream for the future. Maybe it's to be a great dancer. Maybe it's to be a teacher. Maybe it's to be an actor, an athlete, a nurse, a mom, or a business owner. The devil will try to convince you that you aren't enough and that you won't succeed. Those are lies. Learn that now, and be ready when fear tries to whisper in your ear. You can do *anything* God calls you to do because you are emboldened by the fear of God and backed up by the power of Heaven.

Use fear to your advantage. How? By letting it remind you to invite God right into the middle of your fear. We weren't meant to handle moments of discomfort without the presence of God. Those feelings of anxiety can motivate you to turn to God. Release the spirit of fear and embrace the fear of God. You'll find courage, wisdom, and freedom.

YOU CAN DO ANYTHING GOD CALLS YOU TO DO BECAUSE YOU ARE EMBOLDENED BY THE FEAR OF GOD AND BACKED UP BY THE POWER OF HEAVEN.

The spirit of fear doesn't stand a chance with the fear of God as your armor. Dance, sing, speak, teach, fly, soar! Whatever you do, do it with the courage that comes from God. The devil's fear is God's invitation.

Love,

Mom

Miriam

Timeless Loyalty

DEAR DAUGHTER,

I LOVE WATCHING YOU WITH YOUR BABY SISTER. I know she will love you, learn from you, follow you—and probably drive you crazy once in a while.

Your care for your sister reminds me of the story of Miriam in Exodus 2. You've heard me talk about it because it is an especially significant story to me. The Egyptian Pharaoh was terrified that Israel would grow too powerful, so he ordered all the Hebrew male babies under the age of two to be killed, as we saw in the last chapter. When Moses was born, his mother desperately wanted to save his life. She fashioned a basket out of bulrushes, placed her baby inside, and sent him down the Jordan River while Miriam watched from the shore.

By the grace of God, Pharaoh's daughter, the princess,

found him. When the princess opened the basket, the hungry baby began to cry, and the princess immediately felt compassion for him. I can imagine her holding him in her arms, worried about him, and falling in love with him.

Just then, clever Miriam stepped into the picture, acting as if she had just randomly happened to be nearby. She offered to find a Hebrew nurse. When the princess gratefully agreed, Miriam went to get her mother. It was the perfect plan. I'm sure that many years later, when Moses was a national hero, Miriam was proud of the role she played in saving her baby brother from the cruel fate of other Hebrew infants.

Miriam's story doesn't end there. She grew up to become an influential prophetess in Israel. People knew that she spoke for God, and she was held in high esteem by the women of the community. When the Egyptians were pursuing the Israelites on their way to the Promised Land, Moses miraculously parted the Red Sea by the power of God (Exodus 15). As soon as God's people were safely across, the waters closed in over their enemies, destroying all the horses, chariots, and soldiers. Miriam was both a prophetess and a poet, and she led the Israelites in a time of praise and worship, giving God the glory for a victorious end to the battle.

Later, though, jealousy stained her story. She questioned Moses' position in leadership and was more than annoyed with his choice for a wife (Numbers 12). We don't know the details, but clearly, God didn't take kindly to her not trusting His plan. He had placed Moses exactly where He wanted him. Miriam's jealousy brought the curse of leprosy all over her body.

Moses pleaded with God to show Miriam mercy, and God answered His prayer. She had to remain outside the camp for a week, though, as punishment. We see how respected and highly regarded Miriam was within her community because they halted their journey and waited until she could return to join them after she was healed. Not only was she physically healthy again, but I imagine she had a refreshed spirit, no longer carrying greed or jealousy.

> **I FIND MYSELF RELATING TO MIRIAM BECAUSE HER JOURNEY INCLUDES NOT ONLY FAVOR WITH GOD BUT ALSO CORRECTION BY GOD.**

I find myself relating to Miriam because her journey includes not only favor with God but also correction by God. I can think back to times in my life when (I am proud to say) I followed God, loved people, and did what was right—but I can also think of times when (I'm a bit embarrassed to say) I chose selfishness and envy instead of love. As He did with Miriam, though, God has been faithful to lead me, use me, and restore me when I've strayed.

There's another thing that I love about her story: she was by her brother's side their entire lives. As a part of the foster family community, I've witnessed firsthand how quickly children are often forced to grow up and how older siblings can take on the protective role of a parent. I can imagine Miriam and Moses were thick as thieves. Even though she didn't necessarily agree with him at times, her loyalty was commendable. Granted, the leprosy incident wasn't exactly a positive moment in their relationship. Anyone with siblings can probably relate to that kind of conflict, though! And the depth of their love is clear in Moses' immediate prayer for her healing. From that first dramatic rescue at the Nile River through the end of her life, after years of leading Israel together, Miriam was a loyal, supporting, protective sibling to her brother.

Moses' story was actually a huge part of our foster journey long before we ever knew we were going to adopt your sister. That's why you've heard me talk about his story before. Let me explain.

I love to run outdoors. I was not too fond of cross-country in high school, but I find it therapeutic now that I'm an adult. I love to hit the road, get fresh air in my lungs, and spend time with nature for at least two miles in the morning. Sometimes I run on a hiking trail, while other times I run around my neighborhood. I often find myself crossing over creeks or culverts. The air seems to be thinner and cooler around water, so I usually slow down a bit to soak in the temperature difference.

Often when I look down at whatever creek I'm crossing over, I will have a recurring vision of myself discovering a baby wrapped in a dirty blanket, caught in the brush near the water, like a modern-day version of baby Moses. In this vision, my stomach drops, giving me the sensation you might feel if you had arrived at the airport and realized you'd forgotten your wallet. I imagine myself looking around and wondering how no one else has seen the baby. How have they not heard her crying? How has no one found her yet? I envision myself climbing down, clinging onto wet branches as thorns tug at my athletic clothes, and I hear God whisper, "Because you were the one who's meant to rescue her."

As you know, I have an active imagination! But I believe this idea that has appeared in my mind's eye so many times has been God speaking to me. He knew we would someday adopt your sister and that she would be found, safe, and loved with us.

When your baby sister was placed with our family, which would become her forever home, we knew we would give her a name that affirmed her new life and her sense of belonging in our family. I agonized over choosing her name. With you and your brother, I had been dreaming up your names my whole life. But this was different. I wanted her name to mean something as special as her journey into our family.

As I researched B names (because I wanted her to fit in with her new older brother and sister), I came across a name that had a fun ring to it and fit well with Blake and Brax: *Bristol*. But it wasn't until I looked up the meaning behind it that I knew that God had chosen this name for our sweet baby girl. Bristol means "at the bridge." Instantly I remembered that recurring vision on my morning runs.

Here she was. Found. Discovered. Loved. Wanted. Safe.

I pray you would love her fiercely. I pray you would stay by her side, just as Miriam did with Moses. I hope you have the courage and wit to step out of the shadows to defend her when people will—no doubt—question why you look different. Just as I carried you in my belly and you are my daughter, I pray you would remember I carried your baby sister in my heart, and she is just as much my daughter as the children I've birthed. I pray seeds of jealousy would never take root in you, because you trust in God's perfect placement and plan for our lives. I pray you would speak for God and sing out in praise, just like Miriam, thanking Him for all His amazing blessings.

Blessings such as baby sisters.

Love,

Mom

Rahab

Timeless Salvation

DEAR DAUGHTER,

YOU LOVE SUPERHERO STORIES, AND I GET THAT. Who doesn't love to imagine being the strong, brave, beautiful woman who saves the day?

Where do superheroes come from, though? Do you think they know they are heroes ever since they are little girls, playing dress-up in their bedrooms? Do they lie awake at night practicing their superpowers? Do they plan to be heroes when they grow up, or do they become heroes suddenly, almost by accident, when they see a need?

Superheroes aren't real, of course, so we can't really imagine their childhood or know if they wanted to be heroes when they grew up. But in real life, I think heroes often happen more by accident than by choice. None of us are born with super strength or the ability to fly, after all. We are just regular people. We have human problems, real needs, and frequent struggles. And yet, we are all called to help other people. God uses us to "save" one another in small ways and large ways all the time. In a sense, He makes us all heroes.

Here's what is crazy, though. We rarely feel like heroes. We are so conscious of our weaknesses and failings that it's hard to believe God could use us. That's certainly the case for me. I am all too aware of the times I've failed, and sometimes it's hard to believe God could use me.

Maybe that's why Rahab is one of my favorite biblical heroes. Rahab lived in Jericho and assisted the Israelites in capturing the city by hiding two men who had been sent as spies to scout out the land prior to their attack (Joshua 2). Rahab was an unlikely hero. Many times when she's mentioned in the Bible, she's referred to as "Rahab the prostitute." To me, however, she is one of the most courageous women to have ever lived. She's even mentioned in Hebrews 11, the "Hall of Faith," as an example to us all.

GOD USES US TO "SAVE" ONE ANOTHER IN SMALL WAYS AND LARGE WAYS ALL THE TIME. IN A SENSE, HE MAKES US ALL HEROES.

Instead of pretending she was nothing but an innkeeper or judging her in disgust, we need to dig a little deeper into her story. After all, before she was a prostitute who sold her body to men for sex, she was somebody's daughter, somebody's little girl. As a child, I'm sure she didn't daydream about one day growing up and becoming a prostitute. Someone stole her innocence. Someone did vile and evil things to her by robbing her of her purity. Someone close to her, maybe even a family member, might have trafficked her.

At some point, she must have believed the lies that this was the best way to support her family, that her only worth was her body, that she was an object to be used and discarded. I imagine her changing from a daydreaming little girl into a hard, broken woman who would do whatever it took to survive.

Rahab was probably rough around the edges, but she must have also been a good listener. She had heard how God parted the Red Sea, defeated Pharaoh, and performed other miracles to lead His people to the land He had promised them. Somehow, she came to hope that the God of the Israelites could save her, as well. Maybe He could lift her out of her difficult life and rescue her from the cloud of shame and suffering.

Rahab had to choose. Would she live like the people of her city, who worshipped idols made with their hands? Or would she believe the God of the Hebrews, who defends and protects His people? She knew the Lord had given Israel the land. So when the two spies showed up at her house, looking for a place to hide, she felt faith leap in her heart. That faith gave her the audacity to risk her life. She acted quickly, with bravery and decisiveness, taking them to the roof and telling them to hide under some stalks of flax.

The king's messengers knocked on her door. I imagine

her heart began nearly beating out of her chest. "Where are those Israelite spies?" they demanded.

Rahab replied, "The men were here, but they have left the city. If you hurry, you will be able to catch up with them!" (verses 2-5, paraphrase).

Later, after the king's messengers left, Rahab pleaded with the spies to spare her in exchange for her kindness. She even begged them to save her family—the same family that had benefitted from her suffering and who might even have sold her into that life. I believe Rahab was filled with the saving faith of the Spirit. She knew God was the one true God and that only He could save. She couldn't leave her family behind. God's love gave her compassion, and she shared the grace God had shown her with those around her. I believe she was filled with the Holy Spirit to have a heart for the lost who might be left behind.

The spies promised that her family would be safe as long as they stayed inside her home when Israel attacked the city. Then they told her to tie a scarlet rope in her window that would be the sign to Israel to spare Rahab and her family. The spies returned to Joshua and told him how the people of Jericho were melting in fear of the Israelites, saying, "The Lord has surely given the whole land into our hands" (verse 24).

Even though she wasn't an Israelite, God welcomed Rahab into His family because of her faith. The story gets better, though. She later married one of the two spies—who also happened to be a leader, or prince, among his people![1] Rahab went from prostitute to *princess*. As if that weren't enough, she was also an ancestor of Jesus Himself.

WE ARE SAVED, AND WE HELP SAVE. WE ARE RESCUED, AND WE HELP RESCUE.

God rescues those who trust Him. His plan of salvation wasn't just for the people of Israel. God loves people from every nation and wants to bring us all close to Him. And just like Rahab, anyone who trusts God and has faith in His Son Jesus is saved by grace.

This story is a beautiful tale of redemption, but what I especially love about it is how Rahab became a hero for Israel. She didn't let her past failures or her current circumstances define her actions. She decided that she believed God, and she responded in faith to the opportunity before her. God saved her, and she saved her family and Israel.

Do you see how that works? We are saved, and we help save. We are rescued, and we help rescue. Sure, we are weak, and we have some issues in our past, and we don't look or feel like heroes. But God's grace is more than enough.

I can't fully understand the difficult life Rahab lived, the abuse she experienced, or the inhumanity she witnessed. However, I do know we've all had moments when the grace of God has rescued us. Now, it's our turn to help others.

---

1 biblegateway.com, "Rahab," Lockyer's All the Women of the Bible (Zondervan, 1988).

In my own life, I've needed rescuing on more than a few occasions. I remember one time in particular when God saved me from a real pickle. I was nine years old, and I had built up this idea in my mind about how incredibly glamorous it would be to ride the bus. We lived one block away from school, so I simply walked there every day, but I longed to be like my girlfriends who lived out in the country and rode the bus home after school.

One day I concocted a plan. I would tell the bus driver that my aunt, who lived ten miles outside of town, was expecting me for a play date with my cousins. That way, she would let me travel alone. With an uneasy stomach and shaky hands, I climbed on board the bus. The driver believed my lie, and I made my way to the back of the bus, hoping nobody would discover my plan. Riding the bus was everything I ever dreamed of, and I couldn't believe my scheme was working.

Eventually, I heard the bus come to a squeaky halt in front of my destination. I jumped off, skipping to the doorstep as I waved back at the bus. It pulled away, and I watched it grow smaller and smaller in the distance. I had arrived at what was sure to be an incredible afternoon of adventure with my cousins.

I knocked. No answer. I knocked some more. Still no answer. I ran around to the back of the house and banged on the porch door. Nothing. *No one was home!* Oh my goodness gracious! What had I done? How did I get myself in such a mess? My mom was going to strangle me because of my little stunt—if I survived long enough for her to punish me.

Remember, this was 1989, long before cell phones and stricter school protocols. There's no way this would happen today. So there I was, walking alone down the road, ten miles back to town. My mind started spinning stories. What if I passed out from dehydration and died on the side of the road? What if I got kidnapped? What if I got lost forever and never found my way home?

I had no choice but to drop to my knees on the side of the road and pray in a ditch. Even at nine years old, I knew God was the only one who could miraculously save me from this predicament I had caused. Just as I was wrapping up my prayer and about to say amen, I heard truck tires behind me. Thank God it wasn't the boogie man or a kidnapper. It was my Mom's second cousin who had a farm around the bend. He was out checking on sprinklers when he saw me kneeling in the ditch.

"Charla, what in the world are you doing out here?"

I was sobbing. I'm sure he couldn't even understand my story between my rambling words and my gasps for oxygen. I was probably still spinning some web of lies to avoid getting into more trouble. He drove me home, and to this day, I don't know if my parents ever found out I had gotten myself into an impossible situation.

But God knew. He was watching out for me, too.

My little adolescent adventure and my desperate prayer in a ditch pale in comparison to Rahab's story, of course. She was a prostitute turned princess who saved a nation. The common thread, though, is this: if you ever feel like your life is too far gone, like you've strayed from the path, like you're hopelessly lost, God is here to find you. He takes the broken pieces and puts them back together.

That's not all, though. God also uses you to serve and help others. I've had the privilege of sharing some of my own stories of both heartbreak and miracles in front of many people. I'm always amazed how it's my failures, more even than my victories, that seem to speak to people. The grace and salvation of God that are so evident in those failures always encourage people. They know that if God rescued me, He can rescue them.

You see, it's often the very miracle that saved us which God later uses to help other people. One example of this stands out in my mind. It happened a few years ago, just after I had gotten off stage following a speaking engagement in Tulsa, Oklahoma. The most precious girl came up to me. She seemed poised, strong, and vivacious. She was dressed in a brightly-colored sundress and cute boots, and she had a sparkle about her.

IT'S OFTEN THE VERY MIRACLE THAT SAVED US WHICH GOD LATER USES TO HELP OTHER PEOPLE.

I assumed her life was as put together as her outfit, but as we began to talk, I realized she was so overcome with emotion that she was shaking. I held her hands. I could feel how nervous she was and how much courage she had to muster to ask for a photo. She told me how her husband had left her with two kids, one with a severe disability. I couldn't stop the tears from running down my cheeks when she said, "But God is with me."

I marveled at her courage. I could see she had this zest for life even though the wind had been knocked out of her. The world had attempted to dim her sparkle, but she wasn't going to be taken down that easily. She had been broken, but she was redeemed. She found herself on a battlefield, but it was Jesus who carried her across the trenches and through the flying bullets to safety.

Somehow, my story was a tool God used to encourage her. Me? Why me? I've spent more time on my knees in ditches than anyone ever should. I need saving more than anyone!

And that's the point. Superheroes don't save people. Second cousins in pickups do. Faith-inspired prostitutes do. Women and men throughout the Bible and down through history do. You and I do. And most of all, Jesus does.

Love,

Mom

Deborah

Timeless Balance

DEAR DAUGHTER,

I LOVE TO WATCH YOU DANCE IN MUSIC THEATER. You work so hard at learning the steps and songs. Sometimes when you pull off a difficult step, you look around and smile as if the whole world were watching, and your sparkle and joy spill over into my heart and across my face. Other times, when you miss a step or lose your balance, I see your frustration. I know that feeling, too. It's hard to keep everything in your mind at once—voice, movement, timing, music, audience—all while trying to smile and look like you're not terrified that you're going to trip and fall!

You might not dance when you grow up, but you're definitely going to need that same ability to balance everything at once. There will be times when you'll find yourself doing many different things, all at the same time, with a smile lighting up your face, while you secretly wonder if you're capable of pulling it off without falling flat.

That's called multi-tasking, and it's an art every woman has to learn. It requires skill, patience, practice, humor, and a good sense of balance, much like music theater.

Have you ever marveled at a person who has their life together? I'm not talking about someone who just *seems* to have it all together on their social media account, but about a woman who really does everything well. For example, someone who excels in her career, is happily married, is raising exceptional kids, is taking care of herself emotionally and physically, and is strong in her faith in the Lord, all at the same time.

You don't feel pangs of jealousy toward this woman. You might wonder how she does it, but you mostly feel admiration. You cheer her on and hold her in the highest regard. You respect her for all the trials she has been through and how she triumphs over them, stronger than ever. No matter what she faces, she seems to come out on the other side with healthier relationships, a stronger drive for success, and a deeper commitment to God.

Deborah, judge of Israel, was this type of successful, anointed, well-balanced woman. We meet her during the period of the judges in Israel's history, which was after Joshua's death and before Samuel's birth. I've heard this period called the Bible's version of the Wild West. There was no centralized government or leadership. The Bible says everyone did what was right in their own eyes. As we know, doing as we please rather than what pleases God will ultimately lead to our demise. During the period of the judges, Israel was in an ongoing cycle of dysfunction. It was a dark time of chaos and collapse. Over and over, the people of Israel would rebel against God, and He would allow foreign nations to have victory over them. They would then cry out to God and repent, asking for help. God would save them, and for a while, they'd follow Him. But then they would rebel again.

Into this cycle of craziness stepped a woman named Deborah with an anointing from God. Her story is found in Judges 4. Deborah is one of only five women described as a prophet in the Old Testament, and she was the sole female judge. The only other person in the Bible who was said to be both a prophet and a judge was Samuel, many years later.

Deborah had an amazing ability to balance her roles, responsibilities, and relationships. As a judge, the Israelites would seek Deborah's counsel to help them settle disputes. As a prophet, she heard from God and shared His will and vision with others. As a spiritual leader, she could lead worship and preach. And if that weren't enough, she was also a wife and possibly a mother.

The name Deborah in Hebrew means "bee." Just as bees swarm behind a leader, so the people followed this woman who taught and guided them. She gave them organization, leadership, and direction from God. The Bible talks about Deborah sitting under a palm tree, making her counsel available to everyone. She created a welcoming, safe, and healthy environment planted in God's truth.

Talk about someone who wore all the hats! It took a special anointing for Deborah to thrive in unique environments. In your life, you will be called to wear different hats and to be many things to many people. People will pull at you and request things of you until you wonder if your job will ever be done. It takes the strength, spirit, enabling, and capacity of God to thrive in these conditions.

This is especially true when you are the only one like you—maybe because you are the only Jesus-follower in your sphere or because you are the leader everyone looks to for guidance. Think about the unique pressures Deborah faced. She had to operate not only in a male-dominated culture but also in a devil-dominated culture. People had lost all hope, and evil was running rampant in the land. An enemy king, Jabin of Canaan, was making the Israelites miserable, taking away their iron and blacksmiths, leaving them with not even a pocketknife to use as a weapon of defense.

PEOPLE WILL PULL AT YOU AND REQUEST THINGS OF YOU UNTIL YOU WONDER IF YOUR JOB WILL EVER BE DONE. IT TAKES THE STRENGTH, SPIRIT, ENABLING, AND CAPACITY OF GOD TO THRIVE IN THESE CONDITIONS.

In this difficult environment, Deborah called for a man named Barak and told him it was time to bring the enemy's torment to an end. Barak assembled ten thousand soldiers to battle with King Jabin, whose army had far better defenses and weaponry than Israel had. Barak pleaded with Deborah to go with him. He was either terrified or simply had immense respect for her and her leadership. Either way, he felt stronger knowing she would be with his army.

Barak told her, "If you go with me, I'll go. But if you don't go with me, I won't go" (verse 8).

I can imagine Deborah looking at him and thinking, *You're supposed to be the military leader here, but okay. I'll wear another hat.* "Certainly I will go with you," Deborah replied. "But because of the course you are taking, the honor will not be yours, for the Lord will deliver Sisera into the hands of a woman" (verse 9).

When Deborah told Barak that a woman would receive the glory for the victory to come, he probably thought she was referring to herself. But that wasn't in Deborah's character. She was simply doing her part, and she trusted God to decide who received the credit.

DEBORAH IS A BEAUTIFUL EXAMPLE OF A WOMAN WHO KNEW HOW TO MAINTAIN BALANCE IN A CONSTANTLY CHANGING AND OFTEN SCARY WORLD.

It was a long battle, but Barak and the Israelites won. Sisera managed to escape, and he sought rescue in the tent of an unlikely heroine named Jael. She gave him shelter and food, and while he was sleeping, she ended his life with a tent stake through his temple. Gruesome, I know. But the war was over. God had once again saved His people. A woman, Jael, received the glory, just as Deborah prophesied. Because of the courage and anointing from God on both of these women, Israel received new life.

Deborah is a beautiful example of a woman who knew how to maintain balance in a constantly changing and often scary world. While there is a lot we can learn from her, there is one thing that I think made all the difference: she knew how to hear from God about what she was supposed to do, and she operated in that anointing. She didn't try to do everything. She didn't do things in her own strength. She wasn't out to prove anything or to be anybody. Deborah was a real-life hero who saved other lives because she breathed in God's life. She gave wise counsel because she received God's wisdom. She made people feel safe because she knew God's power. She led with confidence because she received God's strength.

I remember a time in my life when I had to turn to God to figure out what He was asking me to do and to receive His strength to do it. At the time, I was building a side business, running my radio and music career, filming a YouTube series, coaching voice lessons, being a mommy to you, and carrying your brother in my tummy, all while keeping my marriage afloat amidst the chaos.

I remember a person who was close to me asking in a rather passive-aggressive tone, "Did *your* mom work five different jobs when she was raising *you*?"

I was floored. Maybe she was trying to tell me I should slow down before I got burnt out. But all I heard was, "You're so high and mighty with all the work you have to do, you should just be a mom and focus on your family." Here I was, working my heinie to the bone, spinning all the plates, trying to be a good mom and wife, and someone dared to call me out on the *busy badge* I was wearing? How dare she!

The words that person spoke drove me to work even harder. They pushed me to do more and be more for everyone around me. I wanted to succeed in everything out of spite, just to prove I could have a happy family and a thriving career. I woke up early, I stayed up late, and I did manage to do it all. I grew that side business faster than any other endeavor I had embarked upon. I rose to the top of the company and became number one in annual personal sales. I raised up other leaders. I mentored and poured into them with every ounce of my soul.

It seemed like I had it all, and I did. Until I just couldn't physically do it anymore. Maybe the words that person spoke over me pulled some kind of reverse psychology trick on me. Or maybe she just saw the path my life was on. She was right, though. I couldn't do it all, and that hurt.

I became exhausted. I was beginning to lose order within my organization. I had fallen victim to some bad counsel and started to see everything I had built begin to crumble. Life felt like a freight train, and I was helpless on the tracks, about to be run over. I concluded that I needed to let go of some of my other passions and simply focus on one thing at a time. With the words, "Did your mom work five different jobs when she was raising you?" ringing in my ears, I decided to set down some of the plates I had tried to keep in motion for years. I didn't want to miss out on the lives of my babies while they were still little. I desperately needed grace and anointing to know what to do and how to do it.

But then, God.

I got quiet and fell to my knees. I prayed for God to counsel me, to give me divine knowledge about how to bring order back into my life. With so much responsibility, I could no longer shoulder it all without Him. I realized I was tired of asking earthly advice without considering what God was saying. I needed to be still and know God was still with me.

I felt so much release when I finally felt His spirit saying, "I've been waiting." I had tried to do it all on my own for so long that I had forgotten what it felt like to have God fighting in my corner. I cried out for an anointing like Deborah.

When I surrendered my finances, career, and family to Him, I was finally able to release the anxiety I constantly felt. It was so hard and so freeing at the same time. I was able to go to bed at a decent hour, sleep well, and wake up with renewed energy instead of constantly feeling drained. I saw God begin to rebuild the relationships I had destroyed because I was too busy to give anybody my whole heart during those years of busyness. God showed me the relationships I needed to nurture, but He also showed me the ones I needed to release because they were not beneficial to me or were giving me bad counsel.

Once my life became proof that my own abilities would fail me every single time, I learned to give everything to God. That has made all the difference. I still love to work. I find fulfillment not just inside my home but outside of it as well. But I no longer try to do everything, and I don't do anything in my own strength. I look to God for direction and wisdom continually.

> **SOME PLATES WILL ALWAYS NEED SPINNING, AND SOME HATS WILL ALWAYS BE ON OUR HEAD. THAT'S OKAY.**

There are a few things we don't have a choice about, of course. As women, we are often a mother, a wife, an employee, a boss, a caretaker, a housekeeper, a tutor, a chauffeur, and much more. Some plates will always need spinning, and some hats will always be on our head. That's okay. We'll look back on these years with fondness, I'm sure. But we don't have to do it all alone, with our own authority and understanding. Instead, we can ask for God's anointing over our lives.

I pray you would never exhaust yourself trying to be everything to everyone, all on your own. I hope you seek the counsel of the Lord, as Deborah did, so that you can be a beacon of hope, safety, and wisdom for others. People and careers will not fill your cup. Busyness will not make you feel better about yourself. Accomplishments won't give you security. Only God can do all that. He can restore your energy, your order, and your well-being by anointing you with His Spirit. He will enable you to rise amidst chaos and dysfunction and to maintain a standard reflecting His grace over your life. He will help you stay balanced, and that's a beautiful place to be.

Love,

Mom

Delilah

Timeless Purity

DEAR DAUGHTER,

I LOVE HOW YOU DO EVERYTHING WITH YOUR WHOLE HEART. When you play, your imagination creates an entire world and makes everything around you fade away. When you are happy, your smile lights up the room like the sun. When you are sad, it's as if the sky has clouded over, bringing gloom and heaviness. When you are mad, you make sure we all know it! Your heart is pure and obvious and clear. There is no mixture or deceit, and I love that about you. You are pure joy, pure passion, pure love.

The word "purity" has to do with being completely the same, through and through. It means you are who you are, without shame, always and everywhere, without hiding anything. To be pure is not to be perfect, but rather to be whole.

Authentic. Honest. The opposite of purity is impurity, which is a word that means mixture or contamination. It implies that something has crept in and spoiled the wholeness.

God wants us to be pure because purity reflects who He is. He is always true to Himself. He is always honest, open, consistent, holy. There is no mixture or contamination in God, which is why living in purity is a recurring message in the Bible. To illustrate its importance, I want to look at a woman who demonstrated the exact opposite of purity: Delilah.

When I started my radio career, a friend and fellow musician who is like a brother to me laughed and asked me, "So now what, are you going to be the Texas country version of Delilah?" Delilah was a popular nighttime radio host whose soothing voice mixed with her distinctive blend of story-telling, sympathetic listening, and encouragement garnered popularity with adult contemporary radio. Her catchy jingle, "De-li-lah!" was famous, so my friend jokingly sang, "Cha-lar-lah!"

I laughed and said, "I'd love to be like Delilah!" I meant the radio host, obviously, because the biblical Delilah was anything but a positive role model. She was a notorious temptress whose relationship with an Israelite man named Samson was certainly not a pure one. As we examine their story in Judges 16, we learn a lot about the harm that comes from deceit, lust, and lies.

Delilah lived in the valley of Sorek, located between the land of the Philistines and Israel. The two nations were enemies. Samson had earned his place as a judge of Israel because of his incredible, God-given strength. He was anointed and called as a warrior for Israel, and his strongman feats were legendary. The Bible tells us that one time, he killed a thousand Philistines with the jawbone of a donkey. On another occasion, when the Philistines tried to lock him in a city so they could kill him, he simply ripped the gate out of the city walls and carried it up a hill, just to prove a point.

The Philistines were desperate to stop Samson. They tried different methods of discovering his source of strength so they could defeat him. Finally, when they learned of Samson's love affair with Delilah, they bribed her with the offer of an enormous amount of money. They knew Samson's weakness lay in the arms of beautiful women. He may have been powerful among men, but he was powerless before women.

Samson was unwilling to choose purity over pleasure. He did not stay true to God's calling or commands. God chose Samson, yet Samson chose the world. He may have been a larger-than-life hero with immense strength, but he lacked restraint and wisdom, and that led to his downfall.

Samson loved Delilah more than his calling and his God. Delilah, on the other hand, loved money more than Samson. She accepted the challenge of finding the source of Samson's strength using cunning manipulation, with seduction and lust as her primary weapons.

For a while, Samson resisted her attempts to discover his secret. He lied to Delilah three times about how he could be captured, and when the Philistines stormed in to take him, he would overpower them with his great strength. He treated his calling like a game or a joke, as if his strength were a gift from God for his benefit rather than a holy calling to serve other people.

Delilah persisted. She wanted the money at any cost. She said, "How can you say, 'I love you,' when you won't confide in me? This is the third time you have made a fool of me and haven't told me the secret of your great strength" (verse 15).

The Bible says that she nagged him "day after day until he was sick to death of it" (verse 16). He gave in and told her the truth: if his hair were cut short, he would lose his strength. Delilah lured him into a deep sleep and had his hair shaved off, and his strength immediately left him. The Philistines quickly captured him, then gouged out his eyes. In a tragic twist of irony, he wasn't just blinded by love and lust, but he was blinded by his captors.

God did not forsake Samson, though. While in prison, his hair began to grow again. One day, when he was being displayed to the Philistine rulers so they could mock him, he prayed for supernatural power once more. God gave him the strength to break the pillars that supported the temple he was in, which caused the roof to collapse, killing him and the people inside. It was a bittersweet end to his life.

Samson's story is a warning to take seriously any temptation that could undermine our purity. I'm not just talking about sexual purity, either, but rather the wholeness and integrity we should display in all areas of our lives. His story is also a reminder to be careful in our dealings with people who are manipulative, vindictive, or caught up in the love of money. Finally, it is an illustration of what can happen if we allow our emotions to be swept up in a heated moment of passion.

What about Delilah, though? What can we learn from her story? For me, her story is a call to purity as well, specifically when we have the power to harm or manipulate other people. It's one thing to be on the receiving end of seduction and deceit, like Samson, but it's another to hurt others, as Delilah did. Both of these things—avoiding temptation and avoiding manipulation—are part of living in purity.

When I met Bryan, the man who would later become my husband, this lesson was front and center in my mind because of the pain I had suffered in the past. I'll share more of this story later, but I had suffered under the thumb of a domestic abuser and predator as a young woman. I knew what it felt like to be Samson, caught up in the fascination of desire and pleasure that another person was using against me. I never wanted to employ those tactics against someone else. I wanted the pure intentions of love to define our relationship, not the selfish intentions of lust.

BOTH OF THESE— AVOIDING TEMPTATION AND AVOIDING MANIPULATION— ARE PART OF LIVING IN PURITY.

Although love and lust are different, they are often confused, so it is important we understand them. Love is selfless and puts someone else's needs above our own. It always thinks about the other person and how to enrich their life. It looks for ways to serve, please, and edify the other person. Lust, however, thinks the exact reverse of love: it is selfish, self-serving, and self-focused. It cares only about what it can get, not what it can give, no matter the cost.

Too many times, I see women use their sexuality to get what they selfishly desire. Even in marriage, women sometimes use sex as a bargaining tool or a source of power over their husbands.

I'm not blaming women for men's lust or lack of self-control, of course. Men must choose to live in purity regardless of their drives, desires, or surroundings. That's on them. I'm also not saying that only men have sexual urges or needs. Temptation and manipulation can flow both ways. I think we all understand that.

What I'm saying here is that Samson had a Delilah, and Delilah must answer for her own selfish actions. I'm speaking to the Delilah tendencies we can all have. We must make sure we are not using our bodies or any other strategy to manipulate people around us for selfish gain.

As a woman trying to get ahead in the man's world of music production, I saw how those tendencies could take over, and I had to resist them. There are subtle tactics that we could employ, such as "innocent" flirting or not-so-innocent sexual favors, to get what we want. That is not love. It is not honest or pure. It is manipulation.

I knew I needed to do some heart work when I met Bryan. I can't explain it, but I knew he was different than anyone I had dated. As we got to know each other, I could sense he had a heart for God, which was what I was looking for. I had made the mistake of getting caught up in relationships with unbelievers before, and I had come to realize there was no use trying to change them. I knew it would be best for me if I were with a man who had Jesus in his heart.

Very quickly, I became overwhelmed with an attraction toward him. I knew I had to pull back on the reins of my flesh. The last thing I wanted was to ruin love by being selfish or manipulative. The funny thing is, I was so determined to be careful that I almost went too far and messed things up!

It happened one night after one of my shows where I was opening for a Texas singer and songwriter at a well-known music venue in South Texas. I invited Bryan to the show. We had been texting back and forth for a while, but this was only the second time we had seen each other in person. After the concert was over, we grabbed a bite to eat at a Taco Cabana.

I didn't want Bryan thinking I was the kind of girl who would kiss on the first date, let alone do anything further. I hoped to make it clear I was a Christian girl looking for a Christian man. When he walked me to my car, he leaned in for a kiss. I wanted to throw my arms around him and dig into a good old make-out session, first because I was attracted to him, and second because I wanted him to know how available I was. But instead, almost without thinking, I ducked my chin, and he was forced to kiss me on the forehead. It was like a "bless you, child" kiss. Awkward, and not exactly what I would have planned.

I was afraid my little stunt had bruised his ego because he didn't contact me for weeks after that. I finally sent him a text. I was driving by his exit on my way to another gig in San Antonio. He replied immediately, and we've been inseparable ever since. We still laugh about the mixed messages I was sending in my desire to be pure.

When I made Jesus the Lord of my heart, He became Lord of my body as well. I freely handed over my selfish desires and laid everything at His feet. I love what Romans 6:13 says: "Do not let any part of your body become an instrument of evil to serve sin. Instead, give yourselves completely to God, for you were dead, but now you have new life. So use your whole body as an instrument to do what is right for the glory of God" (NLT). That means we get to choose how to use our bodies and every other aspect of our beings: for good or evil, for love or lust, for others or self.

It's important to be aware of the power of the human body. As a woman, you are a beauty to behold. You possess great influence, and it can be used for good or evil. You should never be ashamed of your body or feel guilty for your beauty or your sexuality. You simply must decide to continually act with love and wisdom toward those around you, especially your future spouse. Within the context of a committed, healthy marriage, physical attraction and sex are a gift from God to be enjoyed. They are a way to love each other, to serve each other, and to build intimacy and trust.

YOU SHOULD NEVER BE ASHAMED OF YOUR BODY OR FEEL GUILTY FOR YOUR BEAUTY OR YOUR SEXUALITY. SIMPLY ACT WITH LOVE AND WISDOM TOWARD THOSE AROUND YOU.

God gives us beauty to honor Him, not to deceive others for selfish gain. My prayer for your life and relationships is that you would keep the Lord as the foundation. One of the best pictures of marriage ever shown to me is that of a triangle where the wife is at one bottom corner, the husband is at the other bottom corner, and God is at the top. The closer each spouse grows to the Lord, the closer they will grow to each other. The human tendency to use your body or any other tool as a means of control will dissolve when you both seek God first.

As you grow in womanhood, you will become familiar with how much power your body holds. As you grow in faith, you will also learn how to lead your desires toward purity. You'll learn to love, not to lust, and to serve, not to take. Someday, when you find your heart's match, there will be so much beauty! It will be love without manipulation, a mutual commitment to walk through life together. You will be stronger together because you've made God and His love the center of your relationship.

Your pure heart is a gift, and I know you'll use it well.

Love,

Mom

Ruth

Timeless Comfort

DEAR DAUGHTER,

I WILL NEVER FORGET THE DAY YOU WERE BORN. AT 8:47 A.M., your huge eyes and even bigger personality became part of our lives. I was a goner at first sight of you, and so was your dad. At that moment, I had felt I had known you all my life. You were a dream come true and an answer to prayer.

God and I had a little meeting after your birth, though. You see, there was a lot of pain pent up in my heart. By the time you were born, I had gone through some moments of deep hurt. Yes, *you* were an answer to prayer, but not all my prayers had been answered the way I would have hoped, and there were some specific moments of pain that needed to be healed.

I'll tell you a little more about your birth story in a moment, but can we just acknowledge something first? Sometimes, life isn't easy. It can be downright difficult, in fact. All of us face moments of pain, and those moments can affect us in many ways.

Long before your birth, I experienced quite a few of those moments. I was eight years old when our school principal pulled me out of class to tell me my dad would be picking me up early from school. I knew what had happened even without him uttering a word. My Granny, my mom's mother, my best friend, my childhood lifeline, had passed away after losing her battle with aggressive breast cancer. She was only sixty-one years old.

My world was shattered. My little mind could not wrap itself around such loss. I couldn't fathom never seeing her again, sitting on her lap, or hugging her neck. My grief was never-ending. I would cry in my room for hours until I fell asleep. Then, I would have recurring dreams about stuffing myself into an envelope and floating up to space where I might visit Granny in Heaven. My poor mom could hardly grieve the loss of her precious mother because her dramatic daughter kept conjuring up her own plans to go to Heaven. Looking back now, I realize my heart was probably bitter and angry at God. I had come face to face with death and its finality.

Losing my grandmother wouldn't be my only loss early on in my life. Before I even graduated high school, I lost both granddads, comforted a friend when she abruptly lost her dad in a car accident, walked through the darkest time of my life when one of my best friends committed suicide, and more. I still can't believe the number of tears I shed in my youth.

My story is not unique, though. We have all wept over the unexpected losses, injustices, and tragedies of life. Children lose parents, and parents lose children. Loss and pain cannot be avoided. Death and life are intricately bound together. Our individual journeys of loss don't always look the same, but grief is always painful.

I have learned that even in loss—or maybe *especially* in loss—God brings comfort to our souls. I don't know how He does it, and it's not always apparent at the moment, but God is faithful to walk us through the valley of the shadow of death, to comfort us, and to turn our weeping into joy.

Amid the pain, that's hard to remember. We usually have no idea what God is doing through our trials and tribulations. We don't know what the future holds or what good might come from the present evil. All we see is despair.

That is when God becomes most real, though. God sees us in our pain. He weeps with us in our tears. And He gently guides us toward a better future.

The story of Ruth is a beautiful example of God's comfort. Ruth was from Moab, a neighboring nation to Israel. She married into an Israelite family who had fled a famine in Israel. Her mother-in-law's name was Naomi. Over time, Naomi's husband and both of her sons died, including Ruth's husband. That left Naomi, Ruth, and Ruth's sis-

EVEN IN LOSS, OR MAYBE ESPECIALLY IN LOSS, GOD BRINGS COMFORT TO OUR SOULS.

ter-in-law, Orpah, as widows. They were now a family united by marriage, but not by blood; a family stricken with immense tragedy.

They must have thought this was the end of their story. It was only the beginning, though. God was about to turn their bitterness and grief into joy, safety, and love—and an unexpected romance for Ruth.

The day came when Naomi decided she needed to return to Israel. She told both of her daughters-in-law to go back to their families because she had nothing more to offer them. Orpah did so, but Ruth refused. She pleaded with Naomi to let her travel with her: "Don't urge me to leave you or to turn back from you. Where you go I will go, and where you stay I will stay. Your people will be my people and your God my God. Where you die I will die, and there I will be buried. May the Lord deal with me, be it ever so severely, if even death separates you and me" (Ruth 1:16-17).

Naomi agreed, so Ruth and Naomi traveled the long road back to Bethlehem. When they arrived, the women had no food or source of income. To take care of her mother-in-law, Ruth went out to the nearby fields to scavenge the leftover grain after the workers had collected the harvest. She gleaned from a field owned by a man named Boaz. Boaz saw Ruth working diligently to gather food and was smitten by her beauty and her dedication to Naomi. He even told his workers to leave extra stalks of grain for Ruth to find, which was apparently his way of flirting.

When Naomi found out that Ruth had gone to Boaz's field

and that he had shown interest in her, she was overjoyed. Boaz was a distant relative of hers and a very eligible bachelor, to boot. Naomi flew into matchmaker mode. She told Ruth how to approach Boaz and how to discretely hint that she was available as well. The culture of that day was very different, so her actions seem strange to us—but they made perfect sense to Boaz, and he knew he was a lucky man.

To make a long, romantic story short, Boaz and Ruth became husband and wife. Ruth found love in the most unlikely place. She and her mother-in-law no longer had to worry about food or shelter. Eventually Boaz and Ruth had a son named Obed, which made Naomi a grandmother. Many centuries later, Jesus was born to Ruth's descendants.

God took Ruth (and Naomi, too) from heartache to indescribable happiness. Imagine Ruth's pain when she lost her husband, father-in-law, and brother-in-law. Imagine her fear when there was no food, no support system, no hope for a better future. Imagine her loneliness when she first arrived back in Israel. Imagine her hard work to provide for her mother-in-law. Imagine her nervousness as Boaz began to notice her.

Now imagine the overwhelming comfort she found as the pieces of her life miraculously fell into place: romance, love, family, shelter, food, influence, joy, peace, and more. God blessed her for her unending faithfulness to Him, giving her more than she could have dreamed.

I love this phrase, written by King David: "weeping may stay for the night, but rejoicing comes in the morning" (Psalm

30:5). God brings comfort in our sorrow. It might take longer than we wish, and we might go through some pain we never completely forget, but God's grace is always bigger than our loss. His love is always greater than our needs. His sovereign power is always at work to turn what the enemy meant for evil into a blessing.

As I've grown into an adult, I wish I could say that those moments of death and darkness I experienced as a child didn't continue, but I can't. As I noted above, loss is part of life.

One of the hardest trials I've ever faced happened about a year before you were born, when we were practically new-lyweds. We had discovered we were pregnant, and we were overjoyed. We went in for our regular checkup, and things seemed fine. But then the doctor called us back for a follow-up visit. My throat was in my stomach the entire drive. I was afraid something was wrong with the baby.

GOD'S GRACE IS ALWAYS BIGGER THAN OUR LOSS.

My ob-gyn confirmed my fears. She pointed out an abnormal finding on the back of the baby's neck. She laid out all the options, but ultimately told us it looked grim. After weeks of testing, praying, and often bawling in a puddle of tears on the bathroom floor, tests confirmed that the baby had something called Turner syndrome. This condition affects only females and happens when one of the X chromosomes is missing. It can cause various medical and developmental problems, including growth issues, failure of the ovaries to develop, and heart defects.

The sky was falling, and there was no way to stop it. We talked to every professional available to us. We called on every prayer warrior we knew to help us pray for healing over this baby girl inside of me. As we were mapping out plans and ordering every piece of literature known to humanity about caring for a child with disabilities, we faced something far worse. We lost the baby.

The broken heart that my eight-year-old self had pieced back together was now in shards, too tiny to ever repair. A miscarriage or the loss of a baby is a deeper hurt than anyone who has not experienced it could know. My light was gone. There was no color in life, only black and grey.

But then, God.

And my husband. And some dear friends. They all slowly pulled me back into the light. I started to see glimmers of myself again. During this time, though, I pushed God away. We were no longer on speaking terms. He was working inside me, and I can see that now. But at the time, I didn't want to hear about "God's plan" because I was afraid it included more heartache.

When we received a positive pregnancy test three months later, I was hesitant to fully find joy in this news until I knew the baby was healthy. My heart was on eggshells. Every minor spotting or cramp would send me into a tailspin of trauma.

One dark morning just before 5:30, when I was about to jump on the mic for the opening segment of our radio show, I felt the first contraction. The baby was breech, and I remembered my doctor had said to call at any sign of labor. It was time.

My radio co-host walked me to my car and asked me what the date was. I said, "3-13-13."

He replied, "Sounds like a good day to have a baby."

And it was! A few short hours later, we welcomed you into the world. I'll never forget the moment they put you in my arms. Suddenly I couldn't imagine ever having lived without you.

After everyone cleared out of the hospital room, as you lay fast asleep on my chest, just the two of us, I finally decided to have a tough, long-awaited conversation with God. I thanked Him for His blessings. Tears welled up as I asked for forgiveness for turning my back on Him and not trusting His plan. I kissed your head and fell fast asleep in overwhelming peace. Yes, I should have relaxed and leaned into God my entire pregnancy, but I was skeptical. God understood, though. He extended grace and mercy to me in my pain, and He blessed us with you, the greatest gift ever.

God knows our pain, our anger, and our fear. He finds us where we are, and He helps us. He doesn't stand silent in the distance, cold and unfeeling. He doesn't judge us or punish us for our doubts. He doesn't sigh in frustration, wishing we were more patient or mature. He simply comforts us.

My prayer for you is that no matter what pain you face, no matter what valley you walk through, no matter how deeply you are hurt, you would always be comforted by God. Just as He did for Ruth, He will turn your mourning into joy and your sorrow into triumph. And one day, when we meet our loved ones in Heaven, I envision you jumping into your big sister's arms with overwhelming love and joy.

Love,

Mom

Hannah

Timeless Patience

DEAR DAUGHTER,

WE CAN BOTH AGREE ON ONE THING. We hate to wait. I know hate is a strong word, but it's true, right? We hate waiting for websites to load. We go nuts waiting in traffic. Frustration builds if we have to wait in a line for coffee. Our blood boils when we wait for a parking spot to open up. Anxiety bubbles up inside us when we're waiting for an elevator. You especially hate waiting for Opa and GiGi to visit. I've learned not to tell you until moments before they pull in the driveway. Otherwise, the anticipation eats you alive (and drives me crazy).

Can you imagine waiting years or even decades for something? Think about how frustrating that would be—but how wonderful you would feel when you finally saw your dream come true.

Hannah is a beautiful example of someone who endured a prolonged season of waiting (see 1 Samuel 1). She wanted to have a baby for years, but she was unable to become pregnant. It got to the point where Hannah couldn't eat or sleep. She went to the temple in the capital city of Shiloh and cried out to the Lord. Hannah couldn't understand why having a baby, her deepest desire, came so easily to every other woman except her. She made a vow that if God answered her prayer, she would dedicate her child to God, which meant he would serve in the temple.

She prayed so intensely that when Eli, the high priest, saw her, he assumed she was drunk, and he told her to stop drinking so much. Hannah replied that she was simply pouring out her heart to God. Eli, probably a little embarrassed that he had jumped to the wrong conclusion, encouraged her to trust in God: "Go in peace, and may the God of Israel grant you what you have asked of him" (verse 17).

Hannah believed God. She didn't have any guarantees, though, when she wiped away her tears, stood up, and walked out of the temple. She had to continue to wait, just as she had done for so many years. Even though Eli gave her encouraging words, he didn't know the future. He couldn't predict when her miracle might occur. He just told her to let God do His thing, and that was enough for Hannah.

We can learn a lot from Hannah. When she left the temple, her perspective had changed. She ate a meal and wore a giant smile on her face. Maybe for the first time, she realized

God was on her side. She had found peace in the waiting.

The next verse says, "the Lord remembered her." (Well, first it states that she slept with her husband, a detail we probably could have assumed without reading it, but oh well.) That word "remembered" doesn't mean God had ever forgotten Hannah. It means He brought her prayer to the forefront. It means He answered her cry and responded to the desires of her heart.

When the time was right, God gave Hannah the answer to her prayer. And it was worth the wait. She had a baby boy whom she named Samuel, which means "heard by God." Samuel eventually would grow up to be one of the greatest leaders in all of Israel's history.

Waiting is part of life. And yet, we tend to resent it so much. When we are little, we can't wait to be bigger. When we are in high school, we can't wait to move out of our parent's house and go to college. When we are in college, we wish we already had a career and a job. When we have a job, we long for a promotion or a raise, or we wish we could run our own business doing something we love instead of just clocking in and clocking out every day. If we are single, we want the perfect person to hurry up and appear so we can marry them. Once we are married, we can't wait to have kids. We wait for our teenagers to become adults and move out of the house. We wait for our married children to give us grandchildren. Finally, we move to Florida and play golf while we wait to die. How ridiculous! Why do we turn life into a waiting game?

Maybe we focus so much on waiting because waiting is

so frustrating. When you're waiting for Opa and GiGi to arrive, for example, it's hard for you to think of anything else. You get angry if they take too long—and any time at all seems like too long. Waiting can be painful, discouraging, even lonely, and it tends to fill our minds and make us think of nothing else.

The frustration of waiting encourages us to draw closer to God, though. In that sense, it does us a favor. Waiting pushes us to cry out to the Lord, to be honest with Him and with ourselves. Just like Hannah, when we reach the end of ourselves, we find God.

That honesty can be incredibly freeing. Remember, God sees our frustration. He knows our longings. He hears us in our waiting. Hannah brought all her emotions to God, and they didn't scare Him—He responded to them. Our emotions are not a bother to God. They don't offend Him or anger Him or bore

WHEN WE REACH THE END OF OURSELVES, WE FIND GOD.

Him. God already knows our feelings, and He doesn't expect us to always have everything together.

In our waiting, He wants us to know He is preparing the answer to our prayers. As we seek Him and cry out to Him, we should remember that He never stops working on our behalf. We might not see His hand, but that doesn't mean He has forsaken us. It just means we don't have the complete picture.

Brad Levens, a pastor at the church I attend, Creekwood Church, made a statement in a sermon one Sunday that spoke directly to my heart. He said, "God's pace is peace." I love that! Whether you are moving quickly or slowly or not at all, the most important thing is to have His peace. God wants us to experience a state of contentment and rest as He works out the details behind the scenes.

That is easier said than done, though. I have a dear friend whose daughter was diagnosed with a rare disease. The doctors said she only had two years to live. My heart broke for my friend as I watched her wait out the final moments with her child. With each conversation, she would say, "God is with us." While her heart was aching at the thought of losing her precious baby, she was simultaneously in a state of comfort. She knew God was there in the fight with them. That is a true pace of peace.

I can't say I would carry the same strength and peace as my fiercely strong friend. I would be pleading with God or trying to bargain a way around my child's illness. I would cry out for Him to take me instead. My friend found God's peace in the most unimaginable pain, and it gave her strength.

When Hannah bowed in prayer, she made a promise to God: she would surrender her son to Him. I believe that was her way of surrendering herself to God. She was saying that all the desires of her heart, all her goals and dreams, all her pain, all her search for identity and fulfillment now belonged to Him.

My Hannah moment of surrender came when my season working in radio had run its course. Once I started a family, getting up at four in the morning for a radio show or spending days on the road didn't make as much sense as it did when I was in my twenties. When my kids started asking me why I got home in the middle of the night or left for work before they could see me, I knew it was time to move into a profession that provided more time with them, especially while they were little.

It was the hardest choice I've ever had to make. I didn't feel complete peace about my decision for months. I loved my radio career, and music was my entire identity. I remember not even being able to turn on the radio without feeling the sting of jealousy toward my past life as an on-air personality. My throat would drop into my stomach when I saw other female musicians perform—sometimes to the point where it would make me physically ill. I knew I had made the right move for our family. I was grateful for the privilege of being able to stay home, and I loved spending more time with my babies while they were little, but I couldn't understand why my ego was holding on to the life I had left behind.

I cried out to God. I couldn't shake the feeling of resentment over my career move. God had helped me come to this decision, so why did letting go hurt so much? Just as it must have been hard for Hannah to fulfill her promise to give Samuel to the Lord, I struggled with saying goodbye to my life on the radio and my life on the road, traveling with my band, performing in front of crowds of people.

Slowly, God changed my heart. I asked Him to. I could no longer handle the weight of envy and jealousy. My heart began to soften as I surrendered my will and plans for the future to Him. I continue to ask Him to help me in this area because it's a work in process. Part of me still longs to be up on that stage. And who knows what the future holds? Maybe God has some surprises in store. For now, though, I know that I am where I'm supposed to be, and I am beyond grateful for the blessings I've received.

ULTIMATELY, OUR PEACE MUST COME FROM GOD, NOT FROM THE GIFTS HE GIVES.

Today, I have found peace in my decision. I can listen to the radio with a joyful heart. I can be genuinely proud of my girlfriend as she performs in front of adoring fans. I'm constantly in this fluid dance of surrender, and that's where God wants my heart to remain.

Surrendering yourself to God is the best way to live. His ways are the wisest ways, and He is the only one who can give us true satisfaction. There will always be competitions, stages, and awards. Winners will come and go. But the joy that winning and recognition bring is temporary. It fades away as quickly as it came. It's fun in the moment, but ultimately, our peace must come from God, not from the gifts He gives.

I'm sure Hannah missed Samuel, but she knew he had a higher calling. She knew she was doing the right thing. She had the grace to wait for his birth and the grace to surrender his life to the Lord because her heart trusted fully in Him.

By the end of the story, Hannah had at least four more sons. God overwhelmed her with blessings, far more than she asked to receive.

When we wait and trust and surrender like Hannah, the gifts are that much sweeter, and we appreciate them that much more. Hannah's story is a reminder that miracles can happen when we allow God to determine the course of our lives.

God has a unique plan for you, me, and all of us. Once we lay down the competition and comparison, once we silence the voice in our head that says, "that should be me" or "I deserve that," God changes our hearts. When we place our focus on Him rather than on what we've been waiting to receive, things such as fear, jealousy, and despair cannot find a foothold in our hearts because God becomes bigger than anything else. Our prayers change from selfishness to surrender.

In your life, yes, there will be times to wait; but in the waiting, you'll meet God. And yes, there will be times of surrender, but in the surrender, God will overwhelm you with blessings. No matter what season you are in, or what prayer you're praying, or what dream you're pursuing, always remember: His pace is peace.

Love,

Mom

Abigail

Timeless Discretion

DEAR DAUGHTER,

YOU DON'T TAKE NO FOR AN ANSWER VERY EASILY. I'm not saying that you throw fits when you don't get your way or that you whine incessantly. No, you are much smarter than that. Instead, you use your wits, your words, and your will for the win. You find the angles and work them because you know what you want, and you aren't giving up without giving it your best shot.

I can't complain, though, because I'm pretty sure you got your strong will from me. And honestly, your ability to push through opposition in creative ways is a good trait. (Usually, anyway!) I'm glad you are strong. I'm happy you believe in yourself and your opinion. I want you to overcome obstacles in pursuit of what you know is right. I also want you to go to bed on time and get your homework done and limit your screen time, so I will push back when I need to. You might have your dad wrapped around your little finger, but I've got your number!

We all need a healthy dose of that strong spirit and quick mind. As women, especially, doors don't always open easily for us. We need the wit, words, and will to do what we know must be done even when circumstances are less than ideal.

Here's the thing, though. If we use our strength and our smarts only for ourselves, or if we don't know when to fight and when to stand down, or if we can't exercise self-control when necessary, we will end up hurting ourselves and others. That is where discretion comes in. Discretion is the ability to choose when and how to act. It means we have a strong will and clear insight about what needs to be done, but we also have the wisdom, love, and patience to respond appropriately in any situation.

According to German legend, the town of Weisberg was besieged by an enemy king. When he was finally victorious, he condemned the men of the town to death because they had resisted him so fiercely, but he allowed the woman to leave with whatever personal belongings or treasures they could carry. When the time came for the women to go, each one carried her husband, father, brother, or son on her back. Their devotion so moved the king that he spared everyone from death. In memory of this story, there is a beautiful monument near the site of the siege with these words inscribed on it: "A woman's faith."[2]

---

2 D.L. Ashliman. "The Women of Weisberg". 2013. https://www.pitt.edu/~dash/type0875ast.html

It's an inspiring story, whether it's legend or truth. If I were the one composing that inscription, though, I would have added a few more words to the statue. *A woman's strength. A woman's intelligence. A woman's commitment. A woman's absolute determination to find a way where there is no way, so you'd better get out of her way.* Something like that.

There is a woman in the Bible whose story embodies this kind of discretion. Her wit and will are apparent, but so is her wisdom. Her name was Abigail.

In a sense, her story is a real-life Beauty and the Beast tale. When we meet Abigail in 1 Samuel 25, she is married to a man named Nabal. His name literally means "fool" or "′ stupid," and he manages to live up to that meaning in just a few short verses. Nabal was a rich and powerful man, but he was also selfish, mean, and astonishingly unwise. Abigail, on the other hand, was intelligent and beautiful (verse 3).

Now, there is an important backstory here. David (of David-and-Goliath fame) had been anointed by God to become king, but he was currently hiding out in the countryside, running for his life from King Saul, who wanted to kill David to protect his throne. (There's a backstory to this backstory, but I won't get into that here!) While out in the desert with his men, David encountered some of Nabal's shepherds. In that time, it was all too common for thieves to attack shepherds and steal their flocks. David and his men did not harm Nabal's men or steal his sheep, though. Instead, they protected the shepherds from attack.

When it was sheep-shearing time and Nabal was about

to make a profit from the sheep David and his men had helped protect, David sent messengers to Nabal, asking if he would give David some provisions for his men. Not only did Nabal refuse, he insulted David and refused to acknowledge the good David had done.

When David received Nabal's rude response, he lost it. He became outraged. He felt so wronged that he made a rash decision to take four hundred men and fight against Nabal and his lavish estate. It was going to be a full-on war.

One of the servants hurried to Abigail and told her of David's kindness and Nabal's foolish response. The servant pleaded with her to intervene and do something to stop David from killing everyone, saying, "These men have been very good to us, and we never suffered any harm from them. Nothing was stolen from us the whole time they were with us. In fact, day and night, they were like a wall of protection to us and the sheep. You need to know this and figure out what to do, for there is going to be trouble for our master and his whole family. He's so ill-tempered that no one can even talk to him!" (verses 15-17 NTV).

Abigail flew into action. Instead of trying to reason with her husband, she packed up an entire feast and set out to meet David and his four hundred men. She bowed before David and apologized for her husband's foolishness. She gave him the food she had organized, and she begged David not to make a quick decision out of anger that he would regret later and that would displease God.

Abigail's plan worked. Her calm, wise words stopped a warrior in his tracks. David said to her, "Praise the Lord, the God of Israel, who has sent you to meet me today! Thank God for your good sense! Bless you for keeping me from murder and from carrying out vengeance with my own hands" (verses 32-33 NTV). David told Abigail she could return home in peace because he would not harm anyone. With her clear thinking and bold decision-making, Abigail had snapped David out of his anger and saved her entire household.

When Abigail arrived home, she found her husband very intoxicated, so she waited to speak with him. The following morning, she explained how she had saved his life and those employed by him. Nabal was so shocked that he ended up having a stroke and dying a few days later, bring an abrupt and tragic end to his foolishness.

At this point in the story is where David turns from raging beast to handsome suitor. He had clearly been impressed by Abigail's diplomacy and discretion. He knew she had diffused a situation that could have ended in great violence, which would have brought God's displeasure and possibly ruined his future kingship before it even began. When he heard about Nabal's death, he sent his messengers out once again, this time to ask Abigail for her hand in marriage.

Abigail immediately and happily agreed to marry David. Talk about a fairy-tale ending! I can't imagine that she was anything but miserable with Nabal due to his meanness and temper. She remained faithful, firm, and wise, however, and ultimately she was rewarded beyond anything she could have expected.

Abigail has many characteristics that I admire, but her discretion and wisdom stand out the most. She was a thinker, a strategist, and a leader. She knew how to size up a situation quickly and see where

DISCRETION MEANS WE USE OUR WORDS AND ACTIONS TO SAVE, NOT TO HARM; TO LOVE, NOT TO HURT; TO BRING LIFE, NOT TO CAUSE DEATH.

danger might be found. She understood how to respond to anger, misunderstandings, and threats with intelligence and incredible self-control.

Abigail's discretion was the opposite of Nabal's foolishness. He responded rashly, thoughtlessly, aggressively. He almost paid for that with his life and the lives of all his men. Like Abigail, our discretion means we use our words and actions to save, not to harm; to love, not to hurt; to bring life, not to cause death. We are smart, strong, and maybe even stubborn—but we are also wise. We are self-controlled. We are careful with our responses and reactions because we know how much they matter.

There's a saying: "No one ever regrets evil they did not do." Have you ever regretted the words that came out of your mouth? I know I have! All too often, we jump to conclusions and react out of emotions rather than truly thinking things through before we speak. This used to be my greatest character flaw. If someone hurt me, I knew how to drop a bomb of words that would destroy them. I've caused hurt and destruction with my words that I regret to this day.

My father-in-law is a long-time coach and athletic director. He has coached thousands of players and played in hundreds of championship games. All of that experience had made him wise in his speech and careful in his decisions. He recently gave the commencement speech at a graduation ceremony I attended. He said, "Words are like toothpaste in a tube; once you speak them, you can never get them back." Mic drop moment for Richard Barrett, aka PawPaw, aka Ricardo.

A quick wit and cunning sense of humor are helpful skills, but if the words we speak cause other people harm, our skills have become a weakness. If I could go back and reel in some words that poured off my tongue in a moment of rash anger, there are relationships that would still be intact. I've also been on the receiving end of harsh words that I know people later regretted. They didn't regret them in the heat of the moment, but once the dust settled and I distanced myself to avoid further harm, they understood there was no going back to the strong relationship we once shared.

DON'T GIVE FREE REIN TO YOUR MOUTH, BUT DON'T MUZZLE IT, EITHER.

Luckily, as I've grown older, I've found it's easier to hold my tongue. I've also learned to *control* my tongue. There's a difference between those two, by the way. Sometimes you need to be silent, while other times you need to speak, but with control. In other words, don't give free rein to your mouth, but don't muzzle it, either. It's vital to use your voice and have hard conversations when needed. In fact, having those conversations in the right moment can make relationships even stronger by forming a bond of trust and connection on a much deeper level.

I remember one such hard conversation that a friend had with me years ago, when I was still in high school. Growing up in a small town, I had plenty of opportunities to participate in various sports and clubs, including basketball, tennis, golf, track, band, cheer, and drama club. I was sub-par in most of those, to be honest, but I found a good fit with cheerleading and acting. My schedule became insane as I tried to keep up with all the activities I had on my plate.

One day, though, I was cornered in the back of the school bus by a girl I had known since we were kindergarteners. An entourage of three other girls backed her up. She poured out her heart to me about how I had lost myself in all the sports, how I had become stuck up, how running with the "cool girl" clique had made me cold. She told me she thought I had a big shot attitude because I was dating the star quarterback and didn't have time to talk to some of our old girlfriends who used to have slumber parties and build treehouses together.

I was stunned. I remember collapsing on the bus bench in disbelief. I honestly had no idea I had let myself grow into a *mean girl*. It happened so subtly and quickly that I didn't re-alize it until this honest friend was brave enough to snap me out of my selfish ways. I remember we hugged and cried while vowing always to be "besties'" and to include each other in activities in and out of school.

Her honesty hurt, but it was a good hurt, and I was so grateful for her. I know how much courage she mustered up to confront me on such a delicate topic. I marvel at the self-awareness and care she possessed to address me with such calm, gentle words. She opened my eyes to the hurt I had caused and brought me back to a place of humility. To this day, I try to avoid cliques at all costs. If I feel myself slipping into a group that categorizes themselves as "exclusive," I'm out. I want everyone to feel welcome and highly regarded, not rejected or excluded

"Discretion is the better part of valor," goes the old saying. In other words, you don't always have to fight, but you also don't have to give up. A little wisdom and gentleness go a long way. As King Solomon wrote, "Through patience a ruler can be persuaded, and a gentle tongue can break a bone" (Proverbs 15:15).

I pray that, like Abigail, you would have an intuitive and accurate sense of what is right and what is wrong and the insight to know how to respond. I pray that you would be thoughtful, level-headed, and creative in your problem-solving. I pray that you would know when to spring into action and that you would do so boldly, with a strong sense of self. And I pray that you would live with such wisdom

YOU DON'T ALWAYS HAVE TO FIGHT—BUT YOU ALSO DON'T HAVE TO GIVE UP.

that people trust you, seek your advice, listen to your counsel, and follow your leadership.

Never lose your strong will, or your self-confidence, or your ability to overcome obstacles. They are gifts to the world. If you learn to manage them with discretion, motivated by love and led by the Spirit of God, you will be unstoppable. You'll know what needs to be done—and you won't take no for an answer.

Love,

Mom

Bathsheba

Timeless Integrity

DEAR DAUGHTER,

I HAVE A TOUGH TIME BELIEVING GOD CREATED SPIDERS. I feel like somehow they must be a consequence of sin. Their bodies are creepy, their movements are creepy, even their webs are creepy: invisible, sticky traps designed to hold bugs in limbo until they can be eaten alive. That is terrifying.

Here's the thing about those webs. They are built one strand at a time, yet they seem to appear instantaneously. Have you ever noticed that? The kitchen can be spotless when you go to bed, but in the morning, there is a giant web up in one corner, just out of reach. Or you try to move a chair on the patio that you sat in yesterday, and now it's attached to three bushes and a porch column by those tiny death strands.

I could go on, but I'm getting the chills. Here's my point,

though: the lies we tell are a lot like spider webs. Sticky little traps that you hardly even notice until they are fully formed and attached to everything.

Just think about it. Have you ever found yourself in a tricky situation where it seemed like the easiest way out was to tell a lie? Maybe you convinced yourself, "It's just one little lie. How could it hurt?" But that white lie grew into another lie, a mid-sized one this time. Then that lie grew into another, and so on until you ended up with a spider web of sticky, ugly, deathly lies. Unlike our creepy eight-legged nemesis, though, this kind of spider web traps the one who spun it: you and me.

That's how lies work. They are never as easy as they seem. One lie leads to another, and on and on it goes. They take on a life of their own. You fall into a vicious cycle of keeping track of all the lies. At first it is easy to maintain the farce, but soon you feel the weight as your lies start affecting the lives of those around you.

Eventually it all becomes too exhausting to handle, so you come clean. Then everything changes. The weight of your deception is lifted from your shoulders, and things are right in the world. You have apologies to make, of course, and consequences to deal with. However, nothing is as heavy of a burden as the lies your heart had to bear. You wonder why you didn't just come clean in the first place rather than prolonging your agony.

I hate to admit the number of occasions I've told a small lie that grew into a huge, scary monster. Like the time in fourth grade when I didn't do any work at all for our school fundraiser, "Jump Rope for Life." I was supposed to sell trinkets door-to-door to earn a prize. Instead, I stole a twenty-dollar bill out of my mom's top dresser drawer, thinking she wouldn't notice, and turned it in to the school so I could earn a T-shirt or some other prize. But my mom figured it out. Worst of all, she was the elementary school principal at the time. So instead of addressing my theft at home, she called me down to the principal's office, in front of my entire class, and dealt with me there.

Or the time I was working at a country club as an aspiring singer, and the general manager called me into his office to inquire about my talents. He told me he had connections in the industry and asked if I'd bring in the type of songs that were my style. I must have completely misunderstood because I brought in a cassette tape with a few of my favorite artists singing the types of songs I aspired to write one day. The manager thought it was my voice on the tapes and immediately set up numerous meetings with heads of record labels across Music City. I didn't have the heart to tell him it wasn't my voice on the tapes because he was so excited about the possibility of finding a diamond in the rough. I just lived with that all-too-familiar burning in the pit of my stomach until the truth inevitably came out.

I'll also never forget the time I fibbed about graduating from Texas Tech University because I couldn't bear the thought of my boss discovering I had dropped out of college to pursue my musical ambitions. The lie lived on until his daughter asked me to write a recommendation letter because she would be rushing as a Pi Phi for her freshman year of college. Yet again, I had to come clean.

My biggest wake-up call of a lie came when I was caught up in a raw business deal. In that case, the lies were not my own, but my business was directly hurt by them, and I saw other businesses greatly affected.

This dynamic of a lie that grows out of control can be seen in the story of Bathsheba and King David, found in 2 Samuel 11-12. Bathsheba was married to Uriah, a warrior in David's army and one of David's friends and most trusted guards. Uriah protected David when he was hiding in the wilderness, long before he became king.

One evening, while David's men were out fighting a battle, David was resting on his rooftop terrace. While he was enjoying the view and the evening weather, he noticed Bathsheba bathing on her roof, likely as part of a purification process after her monthly cycle. Her exceptional beauty attracted him, so he asked his servants to find out who she was. They told him she was a married woman and that her husband was Uriah. That should have been enough of a warning for David to drop whatever he was thinking. The whole mess that was about to happen could have been stopped right there. But David ignored the warning signs. He sent for Bathsheba and brought her to the palace, and he slept with her.

Here's where the story is a little muddy. We're not sure if David seduced or forced Bathsheba or if Bathsheba was complicit in the affair. Maybe she was a victim, or maybe this was her power play to become part of the royal family. Maybe she loved Uriah deeply, or maybe she was unhappy in her marriage. We don't know. Whatever the context, David got Bathsheba pregnant, and that's where the lies began.

When David found out Bathsheba was expecting, he did everything he could to get Uriah to come home from the battlefield and sleep with his wife so that they could pass the baby off as his. But Uriah was a noble man, and he refused to enjoy the comfort of his house and wife while the army was on the battlefield. Instead, he stayed with the palace troops.

Since that trick didn't work, David came up with another plan, far worse than the first. He sent Uriah back to the battlefield, carrying what was essentially his own death sentence: a note to the general telling him to place Uriah on the front lines of the battle and then to pull back so that Uriah would be killed. The plan worked. Uriah died on the battlefield.

After Bathsheba finished her period of mourning, she and David got married. Now nobody would question the birth of a baby. Problem solved. David had gotten away not just with lies, but with sexual immorality and murder. Or so he thought.

God was angry with David for his sin, for obvious reasons. He sent a prophet to confront David. David repented and pleaded with the Lord for forgiveness. God forgave him, but the baby they had conceived died. The results of David's dishonesty and lack of integrity were deep, far-reaching, and terrible.

Bathsheba later gave birth to a son by David named Solomon. David promised her that Solomon would become king after him, instead of David's older sons by his other wives. God brought good out of evil. He blessed Bathsheba and called Solomon to be king, even though the circumstances that led up to her marriage to David were as dire as you could imagine.

One of the biggest lessons in this story is that God's forgiveness is instantaneous, but consequences can last a lifetime. That's why the choices we make are so important: they have lasting repercussions. For good or bad, the way we conduct ourselves will profoundly affect our lives and the people around us.

Ultimately, we can't really "get away" with anything. Even if nobody else finds out, God knows, and we know. As long as we hide the sin, we live with the weight of a guilty conscience and the terror of being found out. There is nothing easy or fun about that.

David could have stopped this downward spiral at any point. He didn't have to pile lie upon lie, crime upon crime, injustice upon injustice, all in an attempt to avoid the shame of having his sin exposed. We face the same choice: we can admit our lies, acknowledge our sins, and make amends for our failures quickly, rather than

GOD DOESN'T EXPECT PERFECTION FROM US, BUT HE DOES EXPECT INTEGRITY.

getting caught up in a web of deceit that only causes greater pain. It's never easy to come clean—but it only gets harder the longer we wait. Trust me, hiding sin never ends well.

Remember, God doesn't expect perfection from us, but He does expect *integrity*. He wants us to live in a way that matches His image in us, His work in us, and His calling for us. Yes, we'll make mistakes. But there is forgiveness with God. Solomon himself wrote this: "Whoever conceals their sins does not prosper, but the one who confesses and renounces them finds mercy" (Prov 28:13). I wonder if he was thinking about his parents when he wrote that.

The word "integrity" describes a life that is whole, complete, solid, and free from cracks. When a building lacks integrity, it means it has structural damage that could cause the whole thing to come crashing down. In the same way, if we lack integrity, we can't be trusted because we are unstable or compromised on the inside. We might look good on the outside, but we could come crashing down at any moment.

The good news is that repentance brings God's restoration. Even when we've made mistakes, we can repent, turn from our error, and find mercy.

NO MATTER WHAT THE TEMPTATION OR HOW EASY THE LIE SEEMS, NEVER UNDERMINE YOUR INTEGRITY. IT ISN'T WORTH IT. EVER.

David failed significantly, yet God described him as a man who walked "with integrity of heart and uprightness" (1 Kings 9:4). There were real and very painful consequences to his actions, and God didn't take those away. But He forgave David. He continued to bless and use him. Because he was perfect? No, because he admitted his mistakes and returned to his commitment to doing God's will.

David's life presents an extreme example of how lies and covered-up sin can have devastating consequences. Fortunately, most of us won't do anything nearly as dramatic as David. We aren't kings, we don't command armies, and hopefully we aren't wandering around rooftops late at night spying on bathing neighbors. However, no matter how seemingly insignificant a lie or compromise might seem, it always gets bigger. No matter what the temptation or how easy the lie seems, never undermine your integrity. It isn't worth it. Ever.

"The truth will set you free," Jesus said (John 8:32). So, when white lies or small compromises try to get your attention, don't give in. Don't risk hurting yourself or those around you by trying to beat the system. Instead, stop and pray. Search your heart and recognize if seeds of fear, pride, or greed have begun to chip away at your integrity. Come clean before the Lord, and ask for grace and wisdom.

I pray you would have a solid commitment to integrity in your life. I hope you recognize darkness and deceit for the trap they are, rather than falling for their promises of an easy way out. I know you'll live authentically, openly, humbly, instead of striving to look good on the outside but neglecting the inside.

As you grow and learn, as you meet new people and face new situations, and as you make a few mistakes along the way, integrity will lead you and protect you. Honesty will keep your heart at peace. Being quick to tell the truth, quick to repent, and quick to acknowledge mistakes will make people trust you more over time, even if it's less convenient in the moment.

Choose integrity. Build your life on it. Guide your words by it. Shape your actions based on it. Yes, you'll still find cobwebs in your kitchen from time to time. But there won't be any in your heart. That's where it counts.

Love,

Mom

Proverbs 31 Woman

Timeless Consistency

DEAR DAUGHTER,

YOU KEEP ASKING FOR SOCIAL MEDIA, BUT I KEEP PUTTING YOU OFF. I know some of your friends already have phones and social media. You wish you had some way of showing off your dance skills or keeping up with the newest trends—and I keep saying no.

It's not that I don't trust you. There are a few reasons I'm holding off on getting you a phone and social media for as long as possible, but maybe the biggest one is this: I know all too well the pressures that come with scrolling through images of other people, constantly comparing yourself to them. The struggle is real!

As a second-grader way back in 1986, my only worry was if my Skip-It skills would hold up on the playground. Today, you are bombarded with makeup tutorials, hair styling videos, designer outfits, and of course, the latest doodle breed as an accessory. On a more toxic level, you might be exposed to online bullying, explicit language, objectification of women's bodies, and glorification of sex. My head and my heart hurt when I think about the struggles you might face.

The heart of the problem isn't social media, of course. It's us. We are often unprepared to deal with the barrage of thoughts and emotions that come when we start to look around at other people's lives.

I've learned that before I open social media apps, I need to check my emotions and ensure my heart is in the right place. Otherwise, I risk sending my emotions into a tailspin. I know myself well enough to know that if I see other people's lives through my own eyes, I'm likely to feel crushed by the struggles they face, jealous of the successes they have, insecure when their lives seem more put-together than mine, or frustrated that I'm doing laundry instead of vacationing on the tropical beach they're enjoying. Here I am, four decades into my life, and I still have to check myself before I wreck myself on the rocks of insecurity.

The healthiest way to scroll social media (or, for that matter, to do just about anything in life) is to look at other people through God's eyes. I want to feel compassion for their struggles. I want to cheer for their wins. I want to celebrate their endeavors, applaud their advances, and build up their confidence. I want the things I post to make their lives better, rather than just making me look better.

Here's what I try to keep in mind, both online and offline: none of us are perfect, despite what our Instagram feeds portray. All of us are learning, struggling, growing, **LIFE IS LESS ABOUT YOUR HIGHLIGHT REEL AND MORE ABOUT SIMPLY SHOWING UP.** falling, rising again, and pressing forward. That's why the thing that matters most is not how many exotic locations you've taken selfies in, but whether or not you are consistent and faithful in your day-to-day existence. Life is less about your highlight reel and more about simply showing up.

What if social media would have existed in ancient Bible times? I can imagine Ruth rolling her eyes when a video of Naomi pops up, showcasing her latest dance moves in all their glory. I can see Queen Esther posting a picture of her outfit at some lavish royal function. I can envision Mary mindlessly scrolling through her feed while Martha yells at her to help in the kitchen.

Even though we can get a good laugh over that imagery, I'm sure our ancient sisters struggled with the same feelings of inferiority and jealousy we do. Social media is modern, but comparison is as old as Cain and Abel.

Ironically, one of the Bible passages that is meant to celebrate women is often used to do just the opposite. I'm talking about Proverbs 31, that infamous chapter that extols the virtuous woman—and basically makes us all feel like failures in the process. For some reason, this is the chapter that preachers (usually male ones) assume is perfect preaching material for Mother's Day. What makes them think it's a good idea to wave in our faces a list of things we should be doing as women to land the perfect man and be praised by our children? I'm joking. Sort of.

Who is this woman of perfection anyway? Why are we supposed to strive to be like her on the daily? Whoever she is, maybe we should all click the "unfollow" button so her Instagram posts don't trigger feelings of insignificance or insecurity!

Before we cancel the Proverbs 31 woman from our feed, let's find out why God placed her in a Bible story in the first place. The chapter starts off this way: "The sayings of King Lemuel—an inspired utterance his mother taught him" (verse 1). Okay, that really clears things up. Who is King Lemuel?

Some scholars believe that Lemuel was Solomon. Lemuel could have been a name of endearment from his mother. If Lemuel is Solomon, that means Bathsheba would be his mother. Does that mean we're supposed to emulate Bathsheba? The woman who was married to Uriah, the man King David set out to kill so he could claim her as his own? A woman with a past riddled with adultery and scandal? If so, it puts this chapter in perspective just a little. It can't be about perfection because Bathsheba was far from perfect when we first met her.

Even if this wasn't Solomon, and the mother referred to was an unknown historical figure, she was still human. Everyone in the Bible was. That's why we shouldn't just cherry-pick verses, turn them into impossible ideals, and beat ourselves over the head with them. I can imagine this mother dishing out some motherly advice to her son regarding the type of woman he should marry, yet she took a lifetime to hone those attributes. The woman in this chapter is speaking from experience, from lessons learned through trial and error, not because she did everything perfectly the first time. These short verses don't bring up the fact that she probably had decades of failures and false starts to get to a place where she felt comfortable making requirements of what the ideal woman should be like for her son.

Maybe this isn't a list of *to-dos*, but rather a list of *to-tries*. That is, you and I are works in progress. Sure, being a faithful, reverent, strong, well-rounded, charitable, and financially successful woman is an admirable goal, but those qualities are on a spectrum. It's not an issue of "you've got it all" or "you've got nothing at all." Most of us are somewhere in the middle. We're getting better, but we've got a ways to go, and *that's okay*.

As a little girl, I remember finding my mom in a corner of our home with her head in her hands. It was a Sunday, and we had just come from a family lunch at my paternal grandma's house. Mom never said the words aloud, but I knew someone must have made a comment that day that hurt her heart. I had never seen my mom show this kind of vulnerability. It was like she was a little girl and not the vivacious powerhouse that I had always known her to be. I don't know to this day what words were spoken, but I can imagine they were interlaced with Proverbs 31 expectations.

My mother was a working mom of four kids. She was doing the best she could. I'm sure there were many items on her to-do list that never got crossed off. I'm sure there were a lot of things she did that we never noticed, at least not until we were older. But I remember the daily kisses, the hugs before walking out the door, her tucking us in each night, all the braided hairstyles, all the dressing rooms she sat outside as I tried on clothes from Easter dresses to pageant and prom gowns, and the birthdays she made so special for all of her very different children. I still remember her dressing up as Strawberry Shortcake when I turned four—she wore a full costume and pink wig, and the house was dripping in cherry red decorations. She made us a priority every single day.

> LET'S NORMALIZE CELEBRATING NOW, WHEREVER WE'RE AT, BECAUSE WHERE WE ARE AT IS PERFECT.

Mom and Dad raised four very faithful, respectful, strong, well-rounded, charitable, and hard-working children. If the person who made that comment could see us now as successful adults, I wonder if she or he would have a different opinion than when we were rambunctious children, wrecking a spotless house on a Sunday afternoon in our church clothes.

You probably need to hear this as often as I do: we're doing a fantastic, incredible job. We are worth celebrating and congratulating. We don't have to wait until we achieve a state of perfection before we can pat each other and ourselves on the back. Let's normalize celebrating now, wherever we're at, because where we are at is perfect.

I recently heard a speaker refer to our daily tasks as a "ta-da" list instead of a "to-do" list. I love that. What if we celebrated our tiny wins instead of dreading having to do them in the first place? What if we threw a party every time another woman accomplished something on her ta-da list instead of looking at her with eyes of jealousy, comparing ourselves to her highlight reel, feeling inferior and inadequate?

Chasing security by trying to accomplish more is a dead end. We've all proven that, I'm sure. We can never get enough applause, enough Instagram likes, enough expressions of gratitude to "fix" our insecurity forever. Our security must be in God, not in what we accomplish or who notices it. And our focus must be on faithfulness and consistency, not perfection.

I fail at this often because my love language is words of affirmation. So I find myself fishing for praise from my family, friends, and colleagues. I'll scrub the house clean, put away folded laundry, organize drawers, and rearrange the pantry, only for my efforts to go completely unnoticed by my family. I'll say, "How does the house look?" or "Notice anything different?" to which I'll receive a short reply of, "What? Oh yeah, looks great." I have to remind myself my efforts don't go unnoticed by the Lord—even if they go unnoticed by the ones whose messes I am constantly cleaning up!

Career achievements won't give us the inner security we crave, either. I've worked tooth and nail to get a song into the top ten on the music charts, only to find that no one values what I've created. I've crushed goals in my business and gotten my name at the top of the leaderboards. After a while, though, a name loses its luster, and colleagues chalk you up as the "flavor of the month," just another name that will soon fade into oblivion.

In today's comparison-driven world, the only approval that matters is God's approval. If we serve Him, if we live for Him, and if we strive to please Him, we don't have to play the shame game or fall into the comparison trap. Proverbs 31 ends with these verses:

> Her children arise and call her blessed;
> her husband also, and he praises her:
> "Many women do noble things,
> but you surpass them all."
> Charm is deceptive, and beauty is fleeting;
> but a woman who fears the Lord is to be praised.
> Honor her for all that her hands have done,
> and let her works bring her praise at the city gate.
> (verses 28-31)

Yes, her husband and children call her blessed. She even

gets "praised in the gates," which refers to public honor. That's great when that happens—but it can't possibly happen enough to keep our hearts secure. Our confidence tends to leak. If we are depending on our family, friends, and peers to keep that tank full, we're going to drive everyone crazy.

Note one little phrase toward the end, though: she is "a woman who fears the Lord." To fear is to respect. It means to want to please. This woman enjoys the gratitude and praise of the people around her, but she does not depend on that to prop up her self-esteem. She's not trying to impress them. She's serving the Lord. She's pleasing the Lord.

IN TODAY'S COMPARISON-DRIVEN WORLD, THE ONLY APPROVAL THAT MATTERS IS GOD'S APPROVAL.

She cares about God's opinion more than that of any other person. Because she fears and serves Him first, she is free to enjoy the whole process. Her fear of God keeps her steady and consistent. It grounds her. Even when she isn't being praised, she's still confident because her confidence comes from God.

Do you see that? It's not so much about what we do, but the way we do it: faithfully, as if we were doing it for the Lord. *Because we are.* It's consistency and faithfulness to a God who sees everything we do, who loves us no matter what, and who celebrates us daily. If we focused more on serving our families and honoring God rather than seeking approval or trying to impress our friends on Instagram with our perfect posts, don't you think our hearts would be a lot more satisfied and at peace?

IT'S NOT SO MUCH ABOUT WHAT WE DO, BUT THE WAY WE DO IT: FAITHFULLY, AS IF WE WERE DOING IT FOR THE LORD. BECAUSE WE ARE.

In Hebrew, this chapter is an acrostic poem. The first word of every line begins with a subsequent letter of the Jewish alphabet. The author wanted these verses to be easily committed to memory. Why would you need to remember them? Because they are goals, virtues, and attributes we should aspire to *over a lifetime*, not overnight. If you ignore the time factor, you'll throw up your hands in despair and simply give up. Once you understand it's about consistency, though, you are free to celebrate every little milestone of growth along the way.

What if we took the tortoise approach rather than the hare? The point isn't to brag about how fast our progress is, like the hare in the old fable. Instead, let's be more like the tortoise and take life at a slow and steady pace. By the end of our story, over the course of a lifetime, we'll chalk up most or all of the traits of our Proverbs 31 woman. Maybe we'll get a glorious poem about us, written by our husband and children saying, "She is blessed." Maybe not. Maybe they'll just buy us a new air fryer and think that's exactly what we wanted for our birthday. Oh well, God sees, and God knows.

The only opinion you should be concerned about is that

of your Heavenly Father. And you know what? You don't have to work to impress Him. You don't even need to complete your to-do list to find favor in His eyes. You simply need to stand in faith as a believer and let that faith flow out of you through service. He has already accepted you. He has never stopped loving you. He always applauds you.

But for now, while you're living in my house, remember that I'm a work in progress, and I've got a long way to go. So please up pick your dirty clothes before I launch them out of the window. Thank you.

Love,

Mom

Shulamite

Timeless Worth

DEAR DAUGHTER,

I LOVE YOU, AND I LOVE TELLING YOU JUST HOW MUCH I LOVE YOU. "You mean more to me than the world," I'll say, and you'll smile.

I'm guessing that sometime in the next few years, when I say things like that, the smile will be replaced with exaggerated eye-rolls. "I know, Mom, you love me. But could you drop me off a block from school so none of my friends realize I have a mother?"

That's okay. I get it. Fair warning, though: I intend to be the cool mom, so your friends might like me more than you do. Just so you're mentally and emotionally prepared for that.

Even if you roll your eyes, I'm sure that deep inside, you'll know you're loved. You'll know you mean more to me than the world. That's my goal, even more than being the cool mom. I want you to always remember your worth because it's infinite.

It's hard to remember how much you're worth when the world seems determined to tell you how little you matter. It's not just the world out there, either—it's the world inside your head. You can be your own worst critic. You can talk yourself out of believing your own value. I know because I've done it to myself.

When I met your dad, I was a smitten kitten right from the start. I couldn't put my finger on exactly what it was about him, but I had this gut feeling he was *the one*. I gave him my phone number the night a mutual friend introduced us, and I went to bed dreaming about the amazing life we might have together. *Will we live in Austin or closer to our families in north Texas? How many kids will we have? I bet they'll have beautiful dark hair and olive skin tone like him.* On and on, my mind swirled romantically as my puppy-love eyes closed in sleep.

The next morning, though, I made the mistake of conducting an "investigative search" (okay, I stalked him) on social media to get a better glimpse of what his life was like. My lovey-dovey heart sank as I saw photo after photo of him living a life I could never compete with or relate to: enjoying lavish vacations with his family, celebrating his collegiate sports accomplishments, posing with beautiful girls in bikinis, his arms around their sun-

> IT'S HARD TO REMEMBER HOW MUCH YOU'RE WORTH WHEN THE WORLD SEEMS DETERMINED TO TELL YOU HOW LITTLE YOU MATTER.

kissed bodies with their perfect abs.

I began to backpedal in my mind. *There is no way a guy like that could ever love a girl like me,* I told myself sadly. The most extravagant vacation my family ever took was to Amarillo for a two-night stay at the Holiday Inn. I was a college dropout, not a college sports star. And I definitely didn't have a toned and perfectly tanned body like the girls who were his "type."

Just as I was thinking to myself that there was no way he would even date me, my phone pinged. It was him! He asked if he could see me that day. I later found out that on the night we met, he told his mother he had met the girl he would marry. I should have never doubted. I was enough just the way I was.

In the Bible, we learn of a poetic love story between King Solomon and a commoner, a country girl. She did not come from a wealthy family or royal bloodline, yet she dared to profess her love to the king. Others mocked her and reminded her of how unqualified she was. She was embarrassed about how she looked because she had spent long hours in the fields.

The king, though, responded with beautiful words of admiration and acceptance.

How beautiful you are, my darling!
Oh, how beautiful!
Your eyes behind your veil are doves.
Your hair is like a flock of goats
    descending from the hills of Gilead.
Your teeth are like a flock of sheep just shorn,

coming up from the washing.
Each has its twin;
   not one of them is alone.
Your lips are like a scarlet ribbon;
   your mouth is lovely.
Your temples behind your veil
   are like the halves of a pomegranate.
Your neck is like the tower of David,
   built with courses of stone;
on it hang a thousand shields,
   all of them shields of warriors.
Your breasts are like two fawns,
   like twin fawns of a gazelle
   that browse among the lilies.
Until the day breaks
   and the shadows flee,
I will go to the mountain of myrrh
   and to the hill of incense.
You are altogether beautiful, my darling;
   there is no flaw in you.
(Song of Solomon 4:1-7)

The king told her she was perfect just the way she was. With her long, black, curly hair and her straight, white teeth, she was lovely in his eyes. He didn't want to change anything about her.

The Song of Solomon, also known as the Song of all Songs, isn't just a sensual exchange between two lovers. It serves as a metaphor for us to understand how much God loves us and the deep intimacy He invites us to experience with Him.

Though we might feel as if we are inadequate or we don't possess extravagant qualifications, God loves us just as we are. He sees no flaw in us. He

THE LOVE HE GIVES US IS OUR HIGHEST QUALIFICATION

doesn't care if we came from a wealthy family or not, or if we have a college diploma hanging on our office wall, or if we have a perfectly toned body. The love He gives us is our highest qualification. We are His bride, and He is our Bridegroom. This isn't a one-sided love. It's a deep, reciprocated love of pure intentions.

Ever since my mom had a stroke many years ago, I've watched my dad care for her so selflessly. Sometimes I wonder, if I were ever confined to a wheelchair, unable to walk or talk, would your father do what Dad has done as Mom's caretaker? Would he bathe me? Would he blow dry my hair and put curlers in it? Would he help me get dressed and put jewelry on me? Would he take me to get my nails done or to the movies? While I hope we'll have many healthy years together, I have no doubt your dad would give of himself just as my dad has done over the last twelve years of being my mom's primary caregiver.

I adore watching how my dad still looks at my mom. He doesn't see a feeble, disabled woman who is a cancer survivor and stroke survivor. Instead, he looks at her with puppy-dog eyes, just as he did when they met as children. He still sees himself as a poor but witty German boy who is baffled that he snagged the heart of a tall, smart, well-to-do beauty queen. I've never once heard him speak like he was deserving of her heart. It's heartwarming and endearing to watch the exchange between the two of them after fifty-three years of marriage. I'm beyond grateful to have grown up with their example of unconditional love for one another. When she wheels herself into a room in her wheelchair, Dad will sing, "There she is, Mrs. America." Or if she's out of the room, he'll say, "I haven't seen your mom in ten minutes; I'd better go check on her. I miss her."

My mom's "worth" to my dad has nothing to do with what she can do. It's based on who she is: his wife, his sweetheart, his love. The same goes for your dad's love for me, and my love for him, and our love for you. We are worth more than the world because God made us in His image, and He gave us His love. He gave us to each other as well, and He asks us to love one another as He loves us.

Like Solomon and the Shulamite, God desires that we would be in a relationship with Him. We are worthy in His sight. There is nothing we can do to earn His love. We don't need to clean up our past, make more money, lose the extra weight, or drive a nicer car. He wants us to understand just how much He loves us. He has always loved us, and He always will.

I remember coming across a quote that said, "When you look back on your wedding day, may it be the day you loved each other the least." Isn't that true for marriages that last a lifetime? Your father and I definitely love each other more deeply and understand each other more completely than we did the day we were married. I have no doubt my parents love each other more today than they did on that fall afternoon back in 1967 when they said, "I do."

While God can't love us any more or any less because His love is already infinite, we can grow in our *understanding* of that love. The more time we spend with Him and the longer we know Him, the more convinced we become of His love.

Our challenge is to believe that love. It's to accept that God loves us even though we don't have the achievements or qualifications we think we need. Just like the Shulamite, we must accept our King's love rather than trying to earn it.

WHILE GOD CAN'T LOVE US ANY MORE OR ANY LESS BECAUSE HIS LOVE IS ALREADY INFINITE, WE CAN GROW IN OUR UNDERSTANDING OF THAT LOVE.

God declares us worthy, valuable, priceless. He loved us so much that He gave everything for us, including His own Son. That should be enough to convince us that we are secure in Him. God's love will not fade away just because we made a few mistakes or had some bad days. He pursues us with passion and patience because He sees our value even when we can't see it ourselves.

I pray that you would grow in your faith, yielding to an ever-deeper connection with God as you develop your relationship with Him. He longs for you to know Him more, to trust Him completely, and to give Him your whole heart, just as He has done with you.

When He saw you, it was love at first sight. That, my sweet daughter, is the most beautiful love story of all.

Love,

Mom

Jezebel

Timeless Discernment

DEAR DAUGHTER,

I LOVE WATCHING YOU GROW UP. With each passing year, you change: you are taller now, your sense of humor is sharper than ever, and you are more aware of yourself and those around you. You won't be a child for long, and that both scares me and delights me.

As you grow from a girl into a woman, the physical changes that are just ahead are beautiful, but they are not always easy. When I was thirteen, I learned about some of these changes when a friend from Sunday school invited me over for a sleepover. I saw her reach for a box of maxi pads, and I was curious. My precious mother was too modest to explain the process of a monthly cycle, so my girlfriend, who was a few grades ahead of me and much wiser, broke it down for me like this: "You pee blood, and your boobs get bigger."

Fantastic. For the foreseeable future, my expectations about what could happen to my body at any moment now would be based on those few words. I was understandably anxious and terrified until I started my period two years later. Unfortunately, what should have been a time of celebration and the welcoming of womanhood turned into years of shame as I tried to hide the "dirtiness" of what was only natural.

My flat chest sprouted breasts, seemingly overnight. I went from being invisible to capturing the attention of the boys around me—not only in my seventh-grade class, but even those much older. That brought negative attention from other girls my age who were going through the same challenging time but couldn't fathom how I had blossomed so quickly. I still remember the jealous accusations and mean comments directed at me just because I was further ahead than they were in my physical development.

Eventually they concluded I was stuffing my bra. Worse, they decided to expose my tricks—literally. As I was walking to class one day, a girl pushed me into a dark, empty library and ripped open my button-down shirt to see for herself "if they were real." I was mortified, but I was also a little proud that no tissues were filling out my bra, so I showed her my breasts in all their glory. I told her to take the message back to the entourage of mean girls who had put her up to the task of discovering the truth.

What could have been an incident that shut me down or brought out more insecurities actually gave me power. In retrospect, it also opened my eyes to the need for discernment when dealing with other people. I realized that sometimes people's motives can be mean, cruel, and damaging.

Jezebel was a biblical queen who lived many years after the women we've looked at in the last chapters. She ruled during the time of the prophets. She is not a positive example of discernment at all, but rather an illustration of why we need discernment—because people like Jezebel will always exist, and we must be alert and aware.

Jezebel was meanness personified. She appears multiple times throughout the books of 1 and 2 Kings, and we repeatedly read about the deep, negative effect she had on Israel. Jezebel was not just the epitome of a wicked, manipulative, controlling person; she also represents an evil spirit that must be combated with the Spirit of God. That's not to say that my library confrontation with mean middle school girls was a spiritual battle: we were just a group of girls trying to grow up in a world that didn't give us a lot of help along the way. But their meanness, jealousy, and abuse reflect, on a tiny scale, the attitudes that Jezebel demonstrated throughout her cruel reign.

Jezebel was the daughter of Ethbaal, king of the Sidonians and probably a priest of the violent, false god Baal. He was hardly a good father figure. Jezebel was married to King Ahab of Israel, and she was a power-hungry assassin who stopped at nothing to get what she wanted. She was a master over her weak husband, who let her do as she pleased, which included introducing false gods into the land and killing the prophets of the Lord. The worship of Baal was evil not just because it led people to worship other gods besides the one true God, but because it encouraged widespread sexual immorality and terrible violence.

Jezebel's greatest rival was the prophet Elijah, a hero in biblical history. He stood up against Jezebel by inviting her false prophets to a challenge at Mount Carmel. They would see which god—the true God or Baal—would send fire from heaven to burn a sacrifice on an altar. Jezebel's prophets failed to summon Baal after many hours of praying, crying out, and even cutting themselves. Elijah, however, offered up a simple prayer, and God responded with fire from heaven, proving to Israel that He was the true God. Soon after, the Lord then sent a rain that ended a three-year drought.

Elijah had proven the power of the one true God, but because he stood up against Baal worship and encouraged the Israelites to do away with the false prophets, Jezebel was enraged and ordered him killed. He ran from her, afraid for his life. She never found him, though, because God protected him.

That wasn't the only time we see Jezebel's greedy, malicious, and destructive nature on display. In another instance, her husband wanted to buy a plot of land from a man named Naboth, but he refused to sell the land, which was rightfully his and part of his family's inheritance. So Jezebel took matters into her own hands. She ordered Naboth killed. Ahab should have stood up for what was right. Instead, he allowed his wife to "solve" his problems through corruption and violence.

This is the opposite of God's plan for marriage, by the way. Husbands and wives are to support and serve each other toward righteousness, not toward violence. When one spouse is weak, hurting, or simply wrong, the other should help guide that person toward what is right—not find ways to make their wrong attitudes even worse. Ahab and Jezebel were a marriage gone wrong because they aided each other in evil rather than guiding each other toward good.

Ultimately, Jezebel was killed by a man named Jehu, who overthrew her reign and became the next king. Her ending was so gruesome I hesitate to describe it, but the Bible covers it in detail, so I'll at least summarize. When she knew she was about to die, she put on makeup and did her hair. She was defiant, proud to the end, determined to go out as a queen. Jehu ordered Jezebel's servants to throw her from the window to the ground, where she was trampled by horses and killed before her body was eaten by stray dogs. It was a gruesome end to thirty years of tyranny over Israel.

While the story of Jezebel's life and death may be hard to read, it's important to heed the warnings of her life and grow in discernment. We must learn how to recognize people like her and how to avoid becoming like her ourselves. The phrase "Jezebel spirit" has come to be used for someone who will do whatever it takes to get what they want, usually in the pursuit of power. It is an evil, manipulative, vindictive, and selfish approach to life.

That spirit is alive and well in our culture today. Maybe you've come in contact with a Jezebel, or maybe you've encountered a Jezebel spirit within your own soul. A Jezebel spirit isn't limited to women, of course. Anyone can fall for the self-deception of power and greed.

I encountered a full-on Jezebel spirit when I was in the process of growing my business. A woman I know used manipulation and intimidation to take over the lives of my colleagues. One by one, she would form partnerships with humble entrepreneurs. They would grow close, under her control, until she succeeded in swallowing up their businesses and their futures. I would mourn each time I saw another one of her power partners give up on their business and quit their dreams for their life and family. It was more than just eliminating competition that could threaten her business: it was malicious, selfish, and damaging. Her greed had a domino effect on everyone around her. To this day, I don't understand how one person could come in and wreak so much havoc in so many lives.

I grew fearful and anxious as I watched her come closer and closer to my own business. Like Elijah, I wanted to run and hide from her divisive schemes. I was a young leader, and even though I sensed something was wrong, I didn't have the discernment to recognize her motivations and actions for what they were. I felt like a failure because I didn't know how to protect my team against her undoing, and I unknowingly gave her more control by allowing her to continue her evil ways. I would toss and turn at night, unable to sleep. It was like an elephant was sitting on my chest, suffocating and crushing me.

Looking back, I made many mistakes while trying to navigate this disruption. I failed myself and my team. I know there are relationships that may never recover from her wrath. On a few occasions, I tried my own form of manipulation, hoping to regain control of my team. Thankfully, I don't have that same evil nature within me, and it always felt icky. I couldn't keep up with her exhausting, cunning maneuvers.

Eventually, I realized she wasn't merely a vindictive woman—she represented a spirit that only God could deal with. I learned I could not handle Jezebel spirits on my own. I couldn't combat that kind of crazy in my wisdom and strength. I needed the power of God. That was when the elephant on my chest finally got up and left my bedroom. A Jezebel spirit can only be combated by calling on the Holy Spirit. The power of God made all the difference for Elijah, and it does the same for us today.

You cannot stop some people simply by avoiding them or distancing yourself. They will gain momentum in their offensive character and continually cause more chaos. Once I learned I couldn't reason with, educate, or outsmart that level of viciousness, God became my source of hope and defense. I had already blocked her from all contact, but then I fought in prayer, in the name of Jesus, to rid her from my business and my thoughts.

GOD IS MY STRENGTH AND PROTECTOR, AND HE FIGHTS FOR US AGAINST THOSE WHO WOULD TRY TO STEAL, KILL, AND DESTROY.

She finally discovered we would not tolerate her level of evil, and she is no longer involved in our business. I still hear stories of her weaseling her way into conversations, but as for me, I have the armor of God protecting me from her Jezebel spirit. God is my strength and protector, and He fights for us against those who would try to steal, kill, and destroy. I don't know why I had to walk down that path, but I suspect it was to show me how powerful evil can be—and that God is always more powerful. And it certainly taught me to be more discerning, to keep my eyes open for people with a Jezebel spirit.

You will likely encounter Jezebel spirits in your own life from time to time. I'm not talking about jealous pubescent middle schoolers, either, but about people whose way of thinking and acting is completely absorbed with self, with evil, and with power. You usually can't change people like that, and you are never called to stoop to their level.

You need discernment to know if a Jezebel attitude has crept into your own life. Don't accuse people of wrongdoing or be jealous of them just because of their success. Don't fall for the lie that the end justifies the means. Don't manipulate, threaten, and steal your way to the top. Don't sacrifice your integrity for power, wealth, or fame. Don't step on other people as you pursue success. You don't need to because God is with you and He is for you. Let His grace carry you where He wants to take you.

You also need discernment to recognize and reject Jezebels. Don't back down when people are jealous of what you

DON'T STEP ON OTHER PEOPLE AS YOU PURSUE SUCCESS. YOU DON'T NEED TO BECAUSE GOD IS WITH YOU AND HE IS FOR YOU.

have, whether that is your bra cup size or your business success. Learn when to take a stand. Know when to cut off contact or to refuse to allow further damage. Pray, believe, and stand on the promises of God. Keep yourself pure and close to God, as Elijah did. Turn to Him for power and protection for your heart, your family, and even your business.

I pray you would stay pure in your heart by holding tight to God's truth and not your own understanding. I pray that in your pursuit of growth and success, you would act with honesty and generosity, with transparent motives and decisions based on integrity. I'm asking God to give you discernment to recognize a Jezebel spirit if it ever tries to creep into your heart or to attack your life. Most of all, I'm trusting Him to keep you whole and healthy and safe, and to surround you with people who love you.

Starting with me.

Love,

Mom

Naaman's Servant

Timeless Compassion

DEAR DAUGHTER,

THE HARDEST THING IN THE WORLD IS TO WATCH YOU SUFFER. Whether you've fallen and scraped your knee, or you're sad because a friend called you a mean name, or your heart is breaking because you lost something important to you, your pain is real. I feel it, and it makes me sad.

Often, though, I can't take the pain away. Even though I do my best to protect you, there are many things you can't avoid. You must go through them. So I hold you in my arms and talk you through the pain. Eventually you feel better, and you come out stronger, wiser, and more compassionate on the other side. The pain was temporary, but you are a better person because of how you walked through it.

In the Bible, we learn of a young girl from Israel who finds triumph on the other side of great pain and loss (see 2 Kings 5). Her name isn't even recorded in Scripture, and her story is a tragic one at first. Her family was likely killed by the Syrian army. She was carried away from her home by a man named Naaman, who was a mighty warrior and the commander of Syria's army. The girl became a servant to Naaman's wife.

Naaman had a severe, debilitating illness called leprosy. In those days, a person with leprosy would be cast out of their home to live in confinement with others who carried the same disease so they wouldn't infect anyone else. Even though Naaman was held in high favor by the king for the many victories he had won, he remained isolated because of this disease, which began to take over his skin, consume his body with sores, and damage his nerves, breathing, and eyes.

The servant girl knew that her God had the power to heal Naaman. But Naaman had brought great pain and destruction to her family. She could have simply stood back and watched as the disease slowly affected his whole body, and nobody would have blamed her. She could have viewed it as a curse from God because of what he had done to her and her family. Instead, she did the opposite. She felt compassion for Naaman, and she spoke up. She told his wife of a prophet in her land who could heal him: "If only my master would see the prophet who is in

Samaria! He would cure him of his leprosy" (verse 2).

With two simple sentences, this anonymous young woman earned her place as a leading character in an epic story. Her pain, loneliness, and grief are unimaginable. She kept her faith in God, though, and that faith not only guarded her heart through turmoil, but it gave her a spirit of compassion for her master. Her hope in God outweighed her tragedy and her tears. The love of God brought healing to the memories and nightmares of being dragged away from the only life she had ever known.

I can imagine the other servant girls rebuking her for suggesting to Naaman's wife that he travel to see the prophet Elisha. "How dare you share our God?" Or, "What if our God doesn't heal him? Then what? You might be killed!" Not only was she helping the very person who had caused her such great harm, she was also taking a risk by speaking out. That didn't stop her, though.

The girl must have been liked and trusted by Naaman's wife because her words soon reached Naaman's ears. There is such a stark difference between the mighty warrior and the helpless servant girl! They were worlds apart in every way. However, Naaman believed her. I'm sure part of that was desperation, but I wonder if he was also impressed by the genuine compassion of this servant girl who owed him nothing yet cared for his life.

Naaman set out on his journey to see the prophet, bearing gifts worthy of a king. But when he arrived, Elisha didn't even come out. Instead, he sent his messenger with the instructions, "Go, wash yourself seven times in the Jordan, and your flesh will be restored, and you will be cleansed" (verse 10).

To say Naaman was disappointed was an understatement. He was outraged and insulted. Here he was, having believed a mere servant girl, carrying lavish gifts for this prophet who was telling him to wash in a dirty river in Israel. This wasn't what he expected at all. In the middle of his temper tantrum, one of his servants wisely suggested that if Elisha had asked him to do some extraordinary or complicated task, he would have done it. So why not try this simple thing?

To his credit, Naaman listened. He washed in the Jordan River. After the seventh time, he emerged with healthy, clean skin. He was completely cured. He went home to Syria with a healed body and a cleansed soul. He recognized the power of the servant girl's God, declaring, "Now I know there is no god in the whole world, except the God of Israel" (verse 17). Simple words from a servant girl, too obscure to even be named, changed Naaman's life forever. His physical body was healed, and he found a new relationship with the Lord. Naaman's eyes were opened to how powerful God was, and he committed his life to serving Him.

This young girl teaches us so much about walking through pain. She could have become bitter, angry, or hardened. She could have harbored resentment and rage in her heart against the Syrians. Those would have been understandable reactions because of her great suffering. Somehow, though, she found something else in her heart: compassion. Despite the pain and the loss, her heart still beat with the love of God. She was able to see past the injustice and to love those who had wounded her.

I'm sure she still had pain. She still hated the injustice done to her. Her choice to show compassion doesn't excuse the wrongdoing of Naaman and his army or the abuse she had suffered. What happened to her was evil—but she didn't let it control her soul. She didn't allow the pain to close off her heart. Instead, she became stronger through pain. She became more loving through what she had lost. Her heart grew softer and more compassionate because of what she had suffered.

I don't know if I would have done what she did, to be honest. I'm not sure I would have wanted any blessing bestowed on my captor. She had witnessed so much inhumanity, yet she still extended humanity and empathy toward her master. Mercy flowed from her heart because she knew God, and God is merciful and full of love.

While I cannot imagine what she must have felt when she was carried away captive, especially if her family was killed, I have experienced pain and loss. I know the temptation to let those things make you bitter rather than better, smaller rather than larger, vengeful rather than compassionate. And I've experienced how God can bring us through suffering and lead us into a better and brighter future.

I was living in Nashville during the boom of reality television talent shows. Carrie Underwood and Kelly Clarkson had just emerged from American Idol, and Miranda Lambert rose to stardom after appearing on Nashville Star. They went from being struggling artists to selling millions of records with just a few months of national television exposure. So when I earned myself a spot in the top twelve of a network talent show, I thought this was the moment I had been waiting for my whole life.

GOD HAD A PLAN. HE ALWAYS DOES, OF COURSE. SOMETIMES WE'RE IN TOO MUCH PAIN TO SEE IT,

I was told that my time on the show would be close to three months, so I quit my job and rented out my house. We geared up for the premiere with rehearsals, media coaching, wardrobe, and studio time. I was so honored to be a part of the cast, and it seemed as if my music career was finally taking off.

My family and friends couldn't have been prouder, of course. They were going to be on the front row for my big debut at the premiere, wearing T-shirts with my name on them, holding up signs, and shouting encouragement from the audience. Some of them even met the show production staff who came out to document my life for the vignettes that would play before and after my appearance on screen.

We were only days away from the season premiere when a team of producers came to my hotel room. I had lived there for so long that I almost considered it home. They told me to sit down. My heart was racing. My first thought was maybe they would tell me I had already won the show and to play along throughout the remainder of the filming. But they said the opposite. They told me this would be my last day with the show, and I needed to pack my bags right now because a driver would be picking me up in the lobby within the hour.

I couldn't believe what I was hearing. Did I do something wrong? Did they uncover something in my past that would be frowned upon if I won the top spot? I at least wanted an explanation, but none came. To this day, I have no clue why my exit was so abrupt.

When they left, I sat on the corner of the queen-sized hotel bed in complete disbelief. My hope that this show would finally launch my career dissolved in an instant. It was over. It was a disaster. I remember crying uncontrollably as I thought of all the people I would need to contact with the news. I was utterly embarrassed imagining their impending disappointment. I couldn't bear to see my failure reflected in the sad eyes of so many of my supporters. And yet, there was no way around it. Later, I remember screaming into a pillow at a friend's house. I didn't have a place of my own now because I had rented it out. I wished that I had one of those little flashing tools from the Men in Black movies that erased people's memories. Maybe if my family and friends didn't remember I had made it into the cast of a well-known talent show, they wouldn't be disappointed in me when they found out I had been abruptly and inexplicably kicked off it.

But God had a plan. He always does, of course. Sometimes we're in too much pain to see it, and that's okay. God isn't in a hurry. He sits with us in our pain, just as I sit with you.

But unlike me with my motherly attempts to comfort you, God knows the future. He sees what is ahead, and He gently leads us toward it.

For me, that meant moving back home to Texas. I see now that God had been trying to beckon me home on several occasions, but I never listened until I was out of options. It took a hard "no" for me to realize I wasn't where God wanted me in that season of life. That's the real reason I picked up and moved back home. I wanted to say it was because I was too far away from family, but alas, it was because I walked through the ultimate rejection imaginable and had no control over the outcome.

Now I can see the silver lining in the cloud of rejection. If it weren't for my time on the show, I would have never rented out my house, sold my car, or quit my incredible job. God made it exceptionally easy for me to pack up my life in Nashville and go where I was supposed to be. I'm not sure I would have had the courage to shut down everything I had known over the last eight years if it weren't for that abrupt disruption. I would have grown old chasing my music dreams in Tennessee. Instead, God had plans I needed to carry out in my home state of Texas.

When I recognized His divine intervention, I no longer felt shame and disappointment. I felt peace. It didn't matter why a door was slammed in my face by producers of a reality show. I recognized they had opened another door for me, one that led me home. I walked through that door, and I found in Texas what I had not found in Tennessee: favor, grace, influence, success, friends, and a lot of fun. Oh, and your father. I will forever be grateful for all the blessings I've experienced since that defining moment in my music career. A loss that I thought would take my dreams to an early grave turned out to be the birthplace of my career.

Of course, I would be lying to say I responded to my loss with the grace of the servant girl. I was mad at those producers! I was hurt, shocked, and betrayed. I guess I should have had more compassion for the tough choices they were making. Instead, I tried to erase the whole experience from my mind and move on. I cried a lot, though, and beat myself up over it, wondering where I messed up, what was wrong with me, what was wrong with the world. Eventually, it all started to make sense, and I saw the hand of God in my life.

The experience taught me not to waste too many tears on regret. I had to go from a place of *Boo-hoo, poor me*, to *Thank you for removing me from where I never belonged in the first place*, to *What do you have for me now, God?* My loss prepared me for my future. The Lord always has a better future in mind, and while He comforts us in our pain, He knows that we won't stay in that place forever. We will move on, and we will move up. Like the servant girl, the new life on the other side of our pain will often include sharing the com-

THE NEW LIFE ON THE OTHER SIDE OF OUR PAIN WILL OFTEN INCLUDE SHARING THE COMPASSION OF GOD THAT CARRIED US THROUGH OUR SEASON OF LOSS.

passion of God that carried us through our season of loss. As the apostle Paul wrote, "Praise be to the God and Father of our Lord Jesus Christ, the Father of compassion and the God of all comfort, who comforts us in all our troubles, so that we can comfort those in any trouble with the comfort we ourselves receive from God" (2 Corinthians 1:3-4).

You will walk through sorrow in your life. I wish I could always protect you, but I know I can't. However, I find comfort in knowing God goes before you to work miracles on your behalf, and He stays with you in those dark valleys. He will hug you and hold you even when I'm not there. His peace will comfort you. That comfort will expand your compassion for others, and you'll find be a light to people suffering around you even when you're facing darkness of your own. And soon, as you emerge on the other side of pain, you'll find God has led you the entire time.

Love,

Mom

Gomer

Timeless Redemption

DEAR DAUGHTER,

NEVER REALIZED HOW MUCH LOVE MY HEART WAS CAPABLE OF UNTIL I laid eyes on you, my first baby. It was love at first sight, an unexplainable emotion, a kind of love I had never felt before. It was painful and beautiful. It was heart-wrenching and joyful. All these emotions were swirling around me in the hospital room.

Then it hit me. My love for you is a glimpse of how much God loves us. Love is why we call Him Father and why we are called His children. The joys and sorrows a parent feels reflect the relationship the Lord has with us, His daughters.

You are loving, generous, and kind. But I know you are also free-spirited and daring. Like all children, you have curiosity and a zest for life and adventure. That is beautiful, and I would never want to curb your enthusiasm for life.

The problem, though, is that sometimes "enthusiasm for life" can turn into careless or self-destructive behavior. You might fall into that a few times. I sure did! I want you to know that my love for you will never fail or fade, no matter what happens. I knew that the instant I saw your little face for the first time, and I feel the same way today.

If my love as a parent is unstoppably strong, how much stronger is God's love for us? His commitment is eternal, irresistible, unwavering. We fall short again and again, yet the Lord is always faithful. He always forgives. We can never stray too far or go down a road so dark our Heavenly Father can't shine a light on the path that leads back home. Just as a parent waits patiently, arms open wide, for their child to embrace them, so God waits with His loving embrace.

Years ago, I read a novel entitled *Redeeming Love*. The book is a historical romance novel by Francine Rivers set in the 1850s California Gold Rush. I stayed up reading for hours, unable to put the book down. At first, I didn't realize its correlation to the story of Hosea and Gomer in the Bible. It wasn't until I began to recognize the heart of the main character, Michael, and the woman he loved with endless devotion that I realized the novel was based on an incredible story of redeeming love in the Bible.

IF MY LOVE AS A PARENT IS UNSTOPPABLY STRONG, HOW MUCH STRONGER IS GOD'S LOVE FOR US?

Gomer was a prostitute, and Hosea was a prophet. They were an unlikely pair, to say the least. God told Hosea to marry Gomer as a dramatic depiction of how God remained faithful to His people even in their unfaithfulness and self-destructive ways. Hosea took Gomer as his wife, but Gomer kept wandering into the arms of other lovers. She was unfaithful to him. And yet, the Lord told Hosea to go after her and bring her home. One of Gomer's lovers even sold her into slavery, and Hosea had to purchase his wife out of a life of imprisonment. Eventually Gomer had three children, two of whom may have been through other men.

Hosea's faithfulness to his adulterous wife brought God's teaching down to a level the people could relate to and understand. Just as we desire a spouse who would never cheat on us or have an affair outside the confines of marriage, let alone bear children with someone else, the Lord also wants his people to remain faithful, pure, and undefiled.

The Israelites again and again returned to their pattern of worshipping false gods. They were God's chosen people, but they gave their hearts over to another love. And just as Gomer continued to be separated from a husband who loved her, so God's people found themselves lost from God. But He didn't give up on Israel. That's why he told Hosea, "Go, show your love to your wife again, though she is loved by another man and is an adulteress. Love her as the Lord loves the Israelites, though they turn to other gods..." (Hosea 3:1).

Gomer's story is one of constant redemption. The word

"redemption" means to rescue, to buy back, to restore. When we call God our Redeemer, we are saying that He is the one who saves and restores us. He finds us in our sin and error, and He brings us back to Him. We don't deserve it any more than Gomer did, but God's love is relentless.

When we read about Hosea and Gomer, it might be tempting to find ourselves relating more to Hosea: the faithful, loyal, holier-than-thou person who has it all together. We can think back on the people who have wronged and betrayed us, times when we took the high road, refusing to give up, while they went on their selfish ways. Maybe we have been Hosea at times, but at least for me, I find parallels in my life to Gomer.

When I was a young, aspiring musician in Nashville, I fell into unhealthy patterns. My band and I would play gigs in smoky bars, so there was always alcohol flowing around me. I had recently escaped an abusive relationship, and once I discovered I could drink away terrifying memories of abuse, the devil saw an opening to bring destruction to my life. I soon found myself surrounded by "friends" who weren't just drinking; they were using other recreational drugs as a means of escape. Thank heavens that every time someone mentioned drugs, I had flashbacks to my high school anxiety attacks that were brought on by the one time I tried marijuana.

I knew the outcome of drug use was a dark road, but eventually my curiosity got the better of me. One night, after a gig, when we didn't want the party to end, a girlfriend said she was going to meet a friend to "pick something up." It was late (or early, since it was two in the morning), and I didn't want her going alone. When we arrived, her friend made it his mission to make his offer irresistible to me as well. And by irresistible, I mean cheap. Because aside from my moral stance and bad high school experience, one reason I hadn't gotten into drugs was that I was a cheapskate and never want-

HE FINDS US IN OUR SIN AND ERROR, AND HE BRINGS US BACK TO HIM.

ed to dish out the cash it cost to get high. But that night, the things I did were paid for by the devil himself.

That was my one and only hard-core drug experience. After not sleeping for three days, I realized that with my personality, I wouldn't be able to stop if I ever started down that road. The feeling scared me enough to reevaluate everything. I finally had a come-to-Jesus moment where I prayed that He would surround me with people who would push me to live a healthy, balanced life rather than a destructive one. I asked for complete healing from the emotional wounds that the mental and physical abuse had inflicted on me.

I knew I couldn't carry the burdens alone, though. I needed a support system to help me over traumatic hurdles. I quit my bartending job to get away from the constant presence of alcohol and unwanted advances from men, and I started performing at late afternoon writers rounds instead of honky-tonk gigs that went until well after midnight. God was moving the pieces of my life around like a chessboard until I landed where

I needed to be.

Soon I landed a job at a prestigious golf course south of Nashville. Even though I was on staff, I was treated like an equal by the country club members. I met families with the biggest, most generous souls I had ever encountered. I even worked side jobs for many of them, picking up dry cleaning, running errands, cleaning houses, and scrubbing toilets. My schedule became so jammed-packed that I had no choice but to stay on the straight and narrow path. I didn't have time or energy for the devil to slither in with his temptations of drugs or alcohol. I was exhausted in the best way.

My little Girl Friday side hustle grew into a full-time business opportunity. Eventually I opened my own cleaning business called CORNer Cleaners (Get it? CORNer?). I was only twenty-three years old when I left an employee's life behind and began running my own team of workers as the CEO of my first company.

One of the country club members was a contractor who built million-dollar homes, and he hired my company to clean his construction sites. After watching me run a crew and work alongside them, he told me I was too sharp to be scrubbing toilets, and he hired me on the spot to come work in his office on his design team. I still ran my cleaning business on the side, providing jobs for many people, but my new job brought me so much life and joy. Those years working with him as my mentor are some of my most cherished moments in Nashville. My job had nothing to do with music but everything to do with growing into myself and learning how to function in the real world as an adult.

Looking back, if I had never fallen to my knees and prayed for God to change my surroundings, I would not have found myself in an incredible job with a boss who also became a dear friend and advisor. God's gracious redemption and constant love have made all the difference in my life. He never gave up on me, even when I took steps down the wrong path. He was faithful to chase me down, change my heart, and bring me back to Him.

I'm sure that at some point, Gomer was grateful to Hosea for purchasing her freedom from slavery. After she had done him so much wrong by straying from the marriage into the arms of other men, maybe even bearing children who were not her husband's, she never lost his love. Hosea was faithful to redeem her—to buy her back and to bring her back—time after time.

We will hurt God from time to time. That's a sad truth. Whether it's a misguided "enthusiasm for life" or our tendency toward self-destructive behavior, we will stray at times from His ways. Like Gomer, we can become distracted by what the world offers. And yet, the love of our God is even greater than that of Hosea. He will woo us and pursue us to bring us back to Himself.

I pray you would understand the dangers of listening to the lies of the devil and that you wouldn't sell yourself or your future short by pursuing selfish, self-destructive goals in the name of freedom. That kind of life is a dead-end path, and

God wants to keep you free from the pain it brings. I pray you would remain aware of the Gomer tendencies we all have and that you would submit those tendencies to the love and wisdom of God. And I pray that if you do make mistakes, or if you find yourself far from where you know you should be, that you would always turn to God, allowing His grace and faithfulness to redeem you.

His love will be waiting. It will never fail or fade. Because just like me, and far more than me, He fell in love with you at first sight.

Love,

Mom

Esther

Timeless Poise

DEAR DAUGHTER,

YOU HAVE A LOVE-HATE RELATIONSHIP WITH PUZZLES. Well, I think there's more hate than love involved, to be honest. You like the *idea* of puzzles, and the pictures on the box catch your eye, but your attention span is far shorter than the work required to put them together, so your brother ends up finishing them. I get that. Patience is not my strong suit. Maybe that's why puzzles aren't, either.

Here's the thing, though. Life is a little bit like a massive jigsaw puzzle dumped out on a table. It seems impossible to assemble, but God works in mysterious, unseen ways on our behalf to bring all the pieces together perfectly. We don't fully understand until we step back and see the finished result. That's when we realize that God has indeed worked all things together for our good, as Romans 8:28 tells us.

Easton's Bible Dictionary defines God's sovereignty as His "absolute right to do all things according to his own good pleasure."[3] His "good pleasure" is always to do good for us, though, which means that God's sovereignty is a source of great hope and rest for us, especially when the pieces of our lives feel like they're scattered all over the place. Often our journey doesn't make any sense—until it does. Pieces start to fit, a section comes together, images emerge.

Amid all the unpredictability, God helps us maintain balance and peace. Another way of saying that is *poise*. To have poise means to keep your head and your equilibrium even when things around you are changing, and to be ready and prepared for whatever might come. Poise is often used to describe royalty because a ruler should stay clearheaded and calm no matter what happens. A queen with poise might not know everything, but she is confident in her assessment of the situation, self-controlled in her response, and ready to act when the time is right.

OFTEN OUR JOURNEY DOESN'T MAKE ANY SENSE—UNTIL IT DOES.

While God arranges the pieces of life's puzzle, He also enables us to respond calmly and wisely. He gives us poise, not because we have it all figured out, but because we trust

---

3 M.G. Easton, "Sovereignty," Easton's Bible Dictionary (New York: Harper & Brothers, 1893).

Him and are led by Him. We might not see the whole picture, but we can see enough of it, and we trust the One who has our lives in His hands.

The story of Queen Esther is a prime example of God working behind the scenes as all the pieces of her story fall into place. She is probably one of the most popular and highly regarded women in the Bible. Everyone loves the story of an unknown Jewish girl becoming queen and eventually saving her entire people. Interestingly, the name of God is never mentioned in the book of Esther, yet His hand is visible everywhere.

Her story begins with another woman, a true feminist icon named Queen Vashti. Vashti angered King Xerxes of Persia by refusing to obey his drunken command to parade in front of his entire court, probably semi-naked or in a sensual context. This part of the story is an incredible example of standing up for yourself and your rights as a woman.

Back to Esther, though. Embarrassed by Vashti's disobedience, the king kicked her out of her role and went in search of a new queen. He sent out his servants to find the most beautiful women in the land so he could choose one of them to be his new queen. It was basically the first *Bachelor* cast. Maybe you thought ABC had an original idea, but the concept of a lineup of beautiful women competing for a man started around 500 B.C.! All joking aside, though, this could certainly be considered abuse because young girls were pulled from their families, taken to the palace, placed in a year-long program of etiquette training and beauty preparations, and then made to sleep with the king. From there, they became part of his harem.

Esther, whose original name was Hadassah, was among the girls chosen (she took her new name to hide her Jewish heritage). She was an orphan who lived with her cousin Mordecai, who had taken her in when her mother and father died. Something about Esther caught the attention of the king, and he ended up making her his queen. It must have been more than just her beauty because there was a lot of competition in that regard. And as the rest of her story shows, she did have a lot of qualifications. She was brave, wise, and smart, and a true political powerhouse in her own right.

You'll have to read the book of Esther to get the whole story. It's fascinating: full of intrigue, subplots, and bold moves. To sum it up, though, a man named Haman was plotting to destroy the entire Jewish nation. Esther found out about it, but since the king didn't know she was Jewish, and because it was against the law for her to approach him without being summoned by him, she didn't know what to do. Her cousin Mordecai convinced her to go to the king anyway and ask for his help.

Mordecai told her, "For if you remain silent at this time, relief and deliverance for the Jews will arise from another place, but you and your father's family will perish. And who knows but that you have come to your royal position for such a time as this?" (Esther 3:14). Esther agreed to take her request to the king, even though the penalty could be death. She told Mordecai to have the Jewish people fast and pray for three days.

From there, the story gets even more intense. Esther approached the king, uninvited. Instead of having her executed, he welcomed her, which is proof of the influence and respect she had with him. Esther had an entire plan worked out to get the king and Haman into the same room so she could confront Haman in the king's presence. She patiently waited for the right opportunity, then dramatically revealed Haman's plot to exterminate the Jews. The king was furious at Haman. He ended up executing him and enacting a royal decree which protected the Jewish people.

Esther's story is a riveting tale of divine reversal. Like so many of the other stories we've learned from, Esther was an unlikely character whom God used to do miraculous work on behalf of His people. His sovereignty is seen throughout the events in the book. What are the odds that an unknown orphan who didn't come from a wealthy family or have royal blood would become queen? As Mordecai said, God placed her in that role, at that time, to save her people. She couldn't have seen it at the time, but eventually it all became clear.

God arranged the puzzle pieces, but Esther still had to make a choice. She could have panicked and hidden. She could have chosen to remain in the lavish surroundings of the palace chambers, claiming that there was nothing to be done. She could have refused to risk everything to save her people. But she didn't. She kept her head, kept her poise, and kept her promise to Mordecai. Her bravery and wisdom, not to mention her beauty, make her one of the greatest heroes in Jewish history.

As God's daughters, we are called to be prepared for our own "such a time as time this" moments. They are not usually as dramatic and history-altering as saving an entire nation, but that doesn't mean they are insignificant. It could involve showing kindness to a stranger, or standing up for someone who is being abused, or starting a business, or just about anything else that requires poise, bravery, and wisdom. As we take those daily steps in obedience to God, He will bring the pieces of our puzzle together until we see the gigantic, royal calling He has had for us all along.

Remember, Esther didn't start as a queen. God found her where she was at, and He chose her to do incredible things. God finds potential where others feel pity. He sees a queen where others see anonymity. God can work with anything. He doesn't need us to have fame, money, power, or ability. He just needs us to respond in faith to His calling. The quality we must exhibit, like Esther, is the willingness to say, "Lord, I yield my life to you." When we give ourselves to the Lord, we move from disobedience to obedience, from resisting God's plan to trusting God's sovereignty and goodness.

AS GOD'S DAUGHTERS, WE ARE CALLED TO BE PREPARED FOR OUR OWN "SUCH A TIME AS TIME THIS" MOMENTS.

I feel like my life has had its share of Esther moments where I was thrown into an unlikely situation, and I had to make the most of it. There have been times when I was comfortable and happy, like Esther in her palace, only to have a bad person or a difficult situation come along and threaten everything. The entire world was suddenly turned upside down, and everything I thought was certain fell into ruins. But instead of throwing my hands up in despair, I have learned to fall to my knees, to ask others to pray, and to humbly say, "in such a time as this, Lord, use me."

Last year, we decided to sell our house. With a growing family and the possibility that my parents could one day move in so we could care for them in their old age, we crafted a plan. Our goal was to downsize for a while so that we could ultimately build a home that met all our needs. We put our house on the market—and then *boom*, a global pandemic hit and shut down the economy.

Our house had sat on the market for over eight months when an all-cash offer from a precious, elderly couple came through. We rejoiced, thinking this offer was worth the wait. The challenge, however, was that the buyers needed us out in ten days. Even before we went to the title company to close, we packed up the house, found a new home, sold what didn't fit in storage units, and moved you and your brother to a different school closer to the new house. It was stressful, but we were so thankful for the offer that we put our heads down and got it done.

On closing day, we signed the papers. The title company said the buyers' funds were coming from an overseas wire and that we would see the money hit our account by the end of that business day. Five o'clock came, but not the funds. The next day came and went, and we still hadn't seen the cash. Then the next week rolled around, and we still hadn't been funded. By this time, we were getting the runaround from all parties, including the buyers' agent and the title company.

All the documents had been under the wife's name, but eventually Bryan managed to find the husband's full name. A simple Google search revealed this unassuming man in his late seventies was not only a sexual assault offender but a real estate con artist. We had been duped. The money wasn't coming because the money was never there in the first place. Their goal seems to have been to obtain the title of our home, which (thank God!) never happened.

So there we were, paying two mortgages and all the expenses that come with separate houses. That's the last thing our finances needed, especially in the uncertainty of the pandemic. We didn't understand how this was happening to us or what good could come of this. We weren't saving a nation like Esther, so I realize there is no comparison to what she went through. But the emotional, mental, and financial toll was *real*, and it felt insurmountable. I had never seen my husband lose so much sleep, and my anxiety attacks were rearing their ugly head again.

We prayed that God would help us navigate the situation. Lawyers had advised us to sue the couple for money lost, moving costs, and pain and suffering. But we heard the Lord tell us to stay the course. So we put the house back on the market, and God did a miracle. What should have taken months only took a few weeks. A new, legitimate offer came in on the house. It wasn't the best offer, but it was the right offer, and we were finally able to move on from that season in our lives. God pulled a divine reversal out of an impossible situation. In His sovereignty, He protected us from a scam and then guided us to the right buyers, even when the world around us was in chaos.

When you've tried everything on your own and nothing seems to be working, do you have the faith of Esther to call out to God for a divine reversal in your life? Do you have the courage of Esther to rise to the occasion? Do you have the poise of Esther to walk through delicate, difficult times without losing your faith, your temper, or your mind?

Clinging on to God's sovereignty is so much easier than trying to put your own puzzle together. God will use everything for His glory and your good. Let Him be the master of your life. Find peace in His design. If it feels like your situation doesn't make sense, trust God and watch Him bring perfect harmony to your life. For now, you might see more pieces than picture when it comes to the puzzle of your life. It might seem intimidating, frustrat-

WHEN YOU'VE TRIED EVERYTHING ON YOUR OWN AND NOTHING SEEMS TO BE WORKING, DO YOU HAVE THE FAITH OF ESTHER TO CALL OUT TO GOD FOR A DIVINE REVERSAL?

ing, overwhelming. Don't worry. Stay faithful.

Remember, you are here for such a time as this. As you go along, things will fall into place and make more sense. Like Esther, respond with trust and patience, with the poise of a queen who knows she is up to the task. Because with God on your side, you are.

Love,

Mom

Elizabeth

Timeless Mentoring

DEAR DAUGHTER,

I LOVE WATCHING YOU WITH YOUR FRIENDS. I find excuses, such as taking you a snack, just to listen in on your conversations for a moment. Your imaginations run wild as you laugh, play, and talk for hours. I love it so much.

I hope that you always have friends around you. You will need the presence, counsel, and encouragement of other people, including friends and many others. You will turn to family or friends to build fun memories or to share daily joys, as well as to help you through devastating losses. You will look to teachers to instruct you and to lead you into new adventures and untapped knowledge. You will listen to spiritual voices to help you understand the Bible, follow your moral compass, and invest in the most important personal relationship in your life, a relationship with Jesus. All of these relationships and more are mentors in your life. They are there to teach you, guide you, comfort you, and serve you.

The Bible has a lot to say about listening to mentors. However, I find it interesting that there are only a handful of times where women are documented speaking to one another in the Bible. I mean, we girls can talk, right? How are there so few female conversations? Maybe it has something to do with the patriarchal cultures of the day and the fact that all the Bible authors were men. They probably didn't feel comfortable joining in the heart-to-heart convos the women around them were having, which is their loss!

One of the most significant female exchanges mentioned in the Bible was a conversation between two cousins: Elizabeth and Mary, the mother of Jesus. Before we talk about their relationship, though, let's look at Elizabeth's story.

Much like Abraham and Sarah centuries before, Elizabeth and her husband Zachariah had carried a quiet sorrow into their old age because they were childless. Then something unexpected occurred. Her husband, Zachariah, who served in the temple at Jerusalem, was the first person in four hundred years to receive a direct word from God that was recorded in Scripture. While he was burning incense, an angel named Gabriel appeared to him and announced that his wife Elizabeth would have a child who would be named John. The prophecy came true, and Elizabeth became pregnant.

Now, let's fast-forward six months. The same angel, Gabriel, appeared to Mary and informed her that she would conceive by the Holy Spirit and give birth to a son who would be named Jesus. After hearing Gabriel's mind-blowing announcement, I can imagine Mary needed to find someone to talk to about this unique situation as quickly as possible, and she thought of Elizabeth. So Mary decided to visit her cousin.

Elizabeth was the first to recognize Mary as the mother of the Messiah. The Bible says, "When Elizabeth heard Mary's greeting, the baby leaped in her womb, and Elizabeth was filled with the Holy Spirit" (Luke 1:41). Elizabeth immediately understood the divine magnitude of the Messiah's birth.

I can only imagine the joyful time the two expectant mothers must have had as Elizabeth shared advice with her young cousin. Her interaction with Mary distinguishes her as an outstanding mentor. Their relationship reminds me of Titus 2:3-4, "Likewise, teach the older women to be reverent in the way they live, not to be slanderers or addicted to much wine, but to teach what is good. Then they can urge the younger women to love their husbands and children."

Think about Elizabeth's amazing attitude for a moment. She could have been bitter that she waited so long for a child, or she could have grown jealous that Mary, a much younger and less-experienced cousin, was carrying the Messiah. Instead, her generous, mentoring spirit serves as a reminder that God watches over every woman with loving care.

Mary stayed under Elizabeth's care for three months. Around the time she left, Elizabeth's son was born. He would grow up to be John the Baptist, a powerful preacher of repentance and the forerunner who introduced the Messiah.

The relationship between these two women is so encouraging and beautiful. God knew how terrifying it would be for Mary to walk through this journey alone. Even though Elizabeth had to wait patiently into her old age to birth a child, the timing for Mary to have a spiritual mentor who was pregnant at the same time is proof that God's seasons are perfect. He strategically put all the pieces in place. Elizabeth received the answer to her lifetime of prayers, and it happened at the exact time necessary to be a mentor to Mary, who was just beginning her adult life.

DO YOU HAVE AN ELIZABETH WHO CAN HELP WALK YOU THROUGH YOUR THOUGHTS, EMOTIONS, AND DECISIONS?

As a side note, this divine timing also meant that John the Baptist and Jesus were nearly the same age. The Bible seems to indicate that they were also close friends. On one occasion, Jesus said that there was no one greater than John the Baptist, and when John was killed many years later, it had a deep effect on Jesus. The close relationship between Elizabeth and Mary must have contributed to the friendship between John and Jesus as they grew older.

You may not be birthing the greatest miracle in the history of the world, but there's a good chance you are aware of an area or two where you need God's wisdom and strength. Maybe it's a miracle you are praying would come to pass, or a challenge you are facing, or a new opportunity that has opened up for you. How comforting would it be to have a spiritual mentor to talk to? Do you have an Elizabeth who can help walk you through your thoughts, emotions, and decisions?

I've had countless spiritual mentors throughout my life. Some are there for only a short season, while others have remained a constant source of strength for many years. Some mentorships have come in the form of a book, with an author I had no personal relationship with but whose words made a divine impact on my heart. Most of them have been people close to me, and I've been able to learn from their words, their example, and their love.

My husband has been a spiritual leader in our home and a spiritual mentor in my life. We constantly read books together and share Christian beliefs that sharpen our faith. In many ways, our mentoring is mutual because we learn from each other. Where I am weak, he is strong, and where he is weak, I am strong. We lean on each other and depend on each other. I am so grateful for his steadying influence, his wise counsel, and his constant loyalty.

My best friend, Hannah Garber, has also served as a counselor and spiritual mentor. Our friendship has lasted over two decades. We've learned to communicate on deep levels, not only in our friendship but also in business. We recognize how rare of a gift our bond is, and we strive to honor God by challenging one another to continually grow in our faith.

A SPIRITUAL MENTOR WILL TELL YOU WHAT YOU NEED TO HEAR, NOT JUST WHAT YOU WANT TO HEAR.

We are quick to forgive and to show each other grace while holding up God's standards and principles.

I believe these spiritual mentorships have been plentiful in my life because I've always been a very inquisitive person. After too many personal missteps, I started to pray God would put the right people in my path—people I respected and who could guide me in the right direction. Even when I felt like my relationship with Jesus was strong, I still sought outside counsel from people who were willing to share their own experiences of handling challenging situations in a godly manner.

It's important to remember that mentors help you follow God, but they don't take the place of God. They are not infallible, and you must make up your own mind about how you should live. I've received some really good advice over the years—and also some really bad advice. My prayer has always been that God would open my eyes and ears to the voices of truth that I needed to hear. It has not always been pretty, and it hasn't always felt good, because a spiritual mentor will tell you what you need to hear, not just what you want to hear. So don't dismiss their advice just because you don't like it! Listen in humility, pray about it, compare it to Scripture, think through the implications, and in general do your homework. Then make your decision and trust God to continue to guide you.

Remember also that you are called to mentor others. We are both Mary and Elizabeth in this story. You might think you're too young, too inexperienced, or too needy to help others, but that's not how it works with God. We can always receive, and we can always give. Many times, I've found myself called by God to be a spiritual mentor to someone younger. Not in age, necessarily, but in the faith or in some other area. I've been a mentor in business and in spiritual matters, as well as in music, to young girls trying to make their mark in the world with their musical talents.

You may feel ill-equipped to offer up eloquent words over someone's life, but I think you'll be surprised how God will send you a timely message in the perfect moment. You'll look back at your own life and realize how God took you from fearful to fearless. Your story is not for you to keep hidden. No! You've walked through valleys, so you know how to help others navigate their own hardships. Your story of loss may very well be someone else's story of life.

I pray you would seek out spiritual mentors in your life who will help you follow God even more closely. I pray you would be on the receiving end of God-breathed **YOUR STORY OF LOSS MAY VERY WELL BE SOMEONE ELSE'S STORY OF LIFE.** guidance that changes your life because of someone's gift of godly wisdom. And of course, I ask God for your friendships, that you would be surrounded by people who encourage you, challenge you, and make you laugh.

Along with that, though, I pray that you would be a mentor to others. I eagerly anticipate the day when God uses you to bless those around you with your influence and experience. I can't wait to watch you freely pour into others, just as you've been poured into by those who are older or wiser than you. As you grow in your faith, I know you will freely share that knowledge with those around you. May the words you share be a beacon of hope that leads people through life.

I probably won't be able to eavesdrop on you for much longer. And I'm sure your conversations won't always be about puppies and boy bands. You are growing up, and your friends are too. Wherever you go, know that I'll be praying for you: that you would have positive influences and that you would be a positive influence. And of course, I'm always here, ready to talk and ready to listen if you want to chat. Because after all, we girls can talk, right?

Love,

Mom

Mary

Timeless Strength

DEAR DAUGHTER,

YOU ARE STRONG, AND THAT MAKES ME BOTH VERY HAPPY AND A LITTLE BIT SAD. Happy, because I know you'll need that strength. Sad... for the same reason. I wish you didn't have to be strong. I wish I could promise you an easy life, but I'd be lying if I did.

By "strong," I don't mean that you never cry or that you don't show weakness. You certainly know how to tell us when you need help, feel frustrated, or are upset about something. I mean that you know how to get back up when you fall. You understand how to persevere even when things are hard. You are tenacious, resilient, determined.

What you probably don't know is how hard it is for me, as your mother, to watch you face difficult things. I wish I could stand next to you on the dance floor and remind you of the words and the moves. I wish I could go to school with you and face off with the bullies. I wish I could help you take those tests, except I'm terrible at math, and you'd probably do better without me.

You're ten times better at facing difficult things than I am at watching you face them! The way my heart hurts when you hurt makes me think of Mary, the mother of Jesus, and how many times she must have suffered along with her Son. I can't even imagine what that must have been like for her.

Mary played a vital role not just in the birth of Jesus but throughout His life. She raised Him, prayed for Him, encouraged Him, learned from Him, and ultimately, was with Him at His death. Her strength is seen in two ways: first, how she believed and followed God's plan for her *own* life, and second, as the mother of Jesus, watching and supporting Him as He fulfilled God's plan for *His* life.

Can you imagine how Mary, a simple Jewish teenager, must have shaken in terror when the angel appeared to her? An angel named Gabriel delivered the greatest news the world has ever heard, saying, "Do not be afraid, Mary, for you have found favor with God" (Luke 1:30). This ordinary girl was chosen to do the extraordinary.

When Mary heard Gabriel's announcement that she would give birth to Jesus, she replied, "May your word to me be fulfilled" (Luke 1:38). That simple phrase is an extraordinary demonstration of faith and obedience. What she couldn't have known at the time was the tragedy and heartache that lay ahead as Jesus carried out God's plan for salvation. When she gazed at Jesus in the manger, she couldn't know that she would one day gaze at Him on a cross.

Mary had a partial understanding of the pain she would suffer, though. When Mary and Joseph dedicated Jesus in the temple, a holy man named Simeon rejoiced to see Jesus and prophesied that He was the Messiah, but he also told Mary, "a sword will pierce your own soul too" (Luke 2:35). Mary couldn't know what that would mean, but it wasn't long before she began to find out.

Within a year or two of being born, King Herod found out about Jesus' birth from the Magi. In a jealous rage, he ordered the death of all males under two years of age. Joseph and Mary fled to Egypt to save Jesus' life. That was the first time Jesus was in danger of being killed.

The perils of motherhood continued. When Jesus was twelve years old, on a family outing to Jerusalem, His family forgot Him. Mary and Joseph spent three days looking for Jesus. Talk about terrifying! I accidentally locked you in the car one time, and the fire department had to come, lights flashing, and bust you out. It was quite the scene. I can't imagine losing a child for three days, though. They finally found Jesus in the temple, of all places, asking questions and learning about God.

Mary said, "Son, why have you treated us like this? Your father and I have been anxiously searching for you" (Luke 2:48). Personally, I think I would have used stronger language than that!

Jesus calmly informed them that they shouldn't have worried about Him, or at least that they should have known where to find Him. "Why were you looking for me? Didn't you know I had to be in my Father's house?" (verse 49).

Over the years, Mary must have suffered greatly as she saw Jesus threatened and rejected by so many people. He went on long ministry trips around the country, where anything could have happened to Him. He ministered to criminals and outcasts. His life was constantly in danger from the Jewish leaders and the Roman government. All Mary could do was trust God.

OUR STRENGTH GROWS AS WE FACE OBSTACLES AND PERSEVERE THROUGH DIFFICULT TIMES.

Without a doubt, though, the crucifixion was the hardest moment of all. She must have wrestled with God as Jesus suffered and died. I imagine her pleading, "God, I don't understand Your plan as I stand here, watching my Son be wrongly accused, beaten, murdered. My heart cannot take it."

I marvel at Mary's strength. She must have become strong over time, just like each of us does, because our strength grows as we face obstacles and persevere through difficult times. I think her process of growing in strength probably when she responded to Gabriel by saying, "May your word be fulfilled," and soon found herself pregnant. That would have been so difficult. She was young, engaged but still single, with much to learn. I'm sure she was the butt of gossip, jokes, and scorn for becoming pregnant out of wedlock. Fortunately, Joseph was a good man, and he stood with her. But Mary never escaped the rumors of infidelity. Even years later, Jesus was accused of being a child of immorality (John 8:41).

In those early months and years, Mary must have learned to lean into God's promises. Her heart surely returned again and again to the words of Gabriel, Elizabeth, Simeon, and others who had told her who Jesus was and what He would do. She received strength to carry Jesus in her womb, birth Him, raise Him, and send Him into a world that she knew would not always be friendly to Him.

Mary is a beautiful example of the strength of a woman who follows God for her own life and who raises children who will live out God's will for themselves. I can relate to both of those roles. I think all mothers can.

In my own life, I grew in strength through some challenging circumstances. One of the hardest chapters began shortly after I moved to Nashville from Texas when I was nineteen years old. My brother, who had moved there after graduating college, was the only soul I knew. Dad drove me, along with the few belongings I had collected over my short life, the fourteen hours to Music City. There, I planned to realize my dream of becoming the next country music star. I intended to make my family and friends back home proud.

Dad paid my first month's rent, dropped me off at an efficiency apartment, and pulled away. It seemed almost cold at the time, like a quick business transaction between my dad and the unknown future ahead of me. I'm sure I was too excited and giddy about decorating my new little home and planning my road to stardom to notice him wiping away tears as he left his baby girl to fend for herself in the real world.

My dad had always done everything for me, from building dollhouses to mending scraped knees to fixing car tires and changing oil. He was a larger-than-life force no one could ever replace. His expectations were high and his standards even higher. I always wanted to give him something to brag about at the coffee shop, where he would play my music for his buddies. I strived to become the daughter who would make him beam with pride.

When Dad was no longer around, instead of working on a clear-cut plan for achieving my music dreams, I went in search of a father-like figure, someone who could give me a sense of stability in this exciting but scary new world. I didn't realize what I was doing then, of course. It was later, after things went horribly wrong, that I looked back and saw my mistake.

It wasn't long before I found him. Let's call him TDH for "Tall, Dark, and Handsome." He knew everything there was to know about cars—which was the hook, line, and sinker for me. He swept me off my feet with picnics in the park and serenades around the fireplace. He was a smooth talker who moved swiftly into my life. Mere days after my arrival, we were already inseparable. I found out that TDH didn't just know about cars—he seemed to know everything there was to know about *everything*.

Before I knew it, I found myself in an abusive, controlling relationship. He was older than me, and he dropped the hammer in every aspect of my life. He isolated me from friends and family. He put walls up around me. He drove a wedge between any new friendships that started to blossom. It happened so quickly that I didn't see it coming. I didn't notice the warning signs. I didn't recognize the physical, emotional, and sexual abuse. I thought I was inviting it upon myself. I was so young. I was so full of ignorance. And there TDH was, weaseling his way into my innocence, which he took away, too.

I had only lived in Nashville for seven months when I called my parents from a puddle of tears on my bathroom floor. I knew I had to make my escape. I was covered from head to toe in bruises.

Dad said, "Get in your car and drive." He met me exactly halfway, somewhere off the highway near the Oklahoma/ Arkansas state line. I'm sure he pulled out of our driveway at home as soon as he hung up the phone with me. He loaded my little car on a flatbed trailer, and we drove home. He never said, "How could you be so stupid to let this happen?" He didn't say anything. There was just a silent comfort that hung between the two of us as he drove me home so I could heal physically and emotionally.

As a young girl, I was tough. I could handle the messes I had gotten myself into. But now, as a mom myself, I can't fathom the agony my parents must have felt on my behalf as they watched their vivacious, spirited, driven baby girl come hobbling into the house with her tear-stained cheeks and shoulders hunched over in shame. They must have felt like Mary, watching from a distance as their child suffered.

Mary's story encouraged me to have a strength that I didn't believe I had. I saw in her the woman I aspired to be: humble but strong; submitted to God but able to stand up for herself; patient but unstoppable. Over the next few weeks and months, I grew in my walk with God. I found a measure of healing. I began to rely on God like never before.

Now, I look back at that time of entrapment in my life and barely recognize the girl who was caught up in an abusive relationship. It's only by God's grace that I escaped before the wickedness overtook my life. I'm grateful for my parents, who lifted me out of the darkness and loved me through my healing when they easily could have shaken their finger at my mistakes. I'm also thankful for women in the Bible like Mary, who show us how to wholeheartedly trust in God, believing that His plan for our lives is better than our own.

I could have remained in a state of embarrassment and defeat. No one would have blamed me for going into hiding or for abandoning my dreams. But instead, God lifted me out of my shame and made me whole again. You see, I was strong, but not strong enough. And my parents loved me, but their love could only go so far. Ultimately, I needed the strength that only Jesus can bring.

I knew the only way to move forward was to move toward God. The more I grew in my faith in Jesus, the more He increased my confidence to step back into the world.

I surprised myself. I should have been crippled with fear, but I came out of the entire experience stronger. When I first moved to Nashville, I had relied on my own strength and understanding. But when I moved back to Music City, I took with me the armor of God.

Was it easy? No. I struggled for a long time. I found myself looking over my shoulder and wondering if I would run into my predator again. But I fell to my knees in prayer daily and sought the comfort of the Almighty. He gave me the strength to continue.

As a grown woman and a mother, I can't help but admire Mary more than ever for her unwavering faith, even though it must have felt unbearable to carry out God's plan at times. I also admire Joseph, the man she was to marry, who probably couldn't understand how his fiancé was somehow pregnant with the Messiah. In those times, a woman could be stoned to death for carrying a child outside of wedlock. Surely Mary carried an earthly shame and Joseph a questioning heart, even though they both knew she was playing an integral role in God's divine plan. It couldn't have been easy on either one of them. Yet they were both faithful, and God used them in mysterious and glorious ways.

Whether we are facing life for ourselves or watching a loved one struggle through a difficult season, our strength must always be tied to Jesus. Mary herself must have found that strength, and you can too. Remember, Mary started out trusting

God, but eventually she trusted in Jesus, too. At some point, she realized that He was the Savior of the world. He was born to Mary, but He died for the world. God took on human form so He could experience our pain and empathize with the troubles we face. His heart breaks right along with ours in the missteps of life. Like Mary, we must find our strength and hope in Jesus.

You will stumble at times. You will be attacked by enemies who try to rob you of your destiny. That's the way the devil operates. He won't be dressed in fiery red pajamas with horns and a pitchfork. Sometimes he will look like Zac Efron and sing like George Strait. You'll need strength and faith to stand against those attacks. But your strength and my love for you are not enough. You need Jesus' grace and love to get back up and try again.

Jesus is the only one who can bring order and beauty to chaos and confusion. If you've made a mess of things, if life has become so tangled up that you don't even know where to begin to unravel it, give everything over to Jesus. He came to seek and save the lost. Life might leave you vulnerable and heartbroken, but you serve an incredible God of forgiveness who makes you whole again. The apostle John wrote, "In this is love: not that we have loved God, but that he loved us and sent his Son to be the atoning sacrifice for our sins" (1 John 4:10). The strength of a parent is small compared to the strength of your God.

Mary didn't just see Jesus suffer, though. She saw Him triumph over sin, death, and hell itself. She must have rejoiced beyond anything we could imagine when He came back to life. As I look at you now, going about your life with the innocence of childhood, my heart is full of faith for your

JESUS IS THE ONLY ONE WHO CAN BRING ORDER AND BEAUTY TO CHAOS AND CONFUSION.

future. Yes, I dread the moments of heartbreak that will undoubtedly come, but I look forward to the victories and the joy that I know will be yours. You are strong, my daughter, and you have Jesus by your side. That is all you need.

Love,

Mom

Anna

Timeless Devotion

DEAR DAUGHTER,

YOU AREN'T A TEENAGER YET, which means you have not yet adopted the standard teenager habit of continually reminding your parents how old they are. Those days are coming, though. It's just a matter of time.

I'm sure you'll always think I'm old—right up until you have kids of your own. That's when you suddenly realize that adults are not old. Kids are *young*. When you were born, I became painfully aware of how unprepared I was to be a mother. Suddenly age wasn't just a number, it was a sign of experience. Of wisdom. Of trustworthiness. That's why you need older women in your life, both now and for many years to come. (I'm not sure I like to describe myself as an "older woman" since I'm barely forty years old, but hey, I'm sure you would. So I'm just going to run with that.)

When I was a little girl, even younger than you are now, my parents volunteered to be directors of the seniors ministry in our small-town Baptist church. I still remember Mom and Dad loading us four kids and thirty or so older adults into the church's white recreational bus and setting out on a day trip to Amarillo to see the grand Christmas tree and pageant. We were scattered about the bus, sitting on the laps of various grandparents who didn't belong to us, but we loved them dearly. After the hour-and-a-half drive, we cruised through the nearby neighborhoods to *ooh* and *ahh* over the gleaming holiday lights strung on houses.

Then came my favorite part: eating at Luby's Cafeteria, where seniors ate almost for free. Oh, Luby's, such sacred ground! My parents still laugh out loud when they tell the story about each of us went through the cafeteria line with a different elderly couple and sat at different tables, yet we all ended up with steaming piles of liver and onions on our plates. Mom and Dad raised us right! From an early age, we learned to honor the elderly—and to value good, wholesome, southern cooking.

I didn't want the adventure to end, but eventually we made the long trek back home. I remember dozing off on the warm church bus floor next to rows of polished shoes, my heart full after a day of holiday cheer with some of my favorite people.

My connection with several of the seniors didn't stop at church. When most other little girls were out climbing trees or riding bikes with their friends, you would often find me at the home of an elderly widow, learning how to crochet, play cards, or sew Barbie doll clothes. These women were my besties. I loved hearing their stories about life, love, and loss. I know they loved my company, too,

GOD DELIGHTS IN USING PEOPLE THE WORLD THINKS ARE NOBODIES.

and I could feel their prayers over my life. My visits became less frequent as I grew into a teenager with a full schedule of sports and extracurricular activities. One by one, they went to be with the Lord, and I grieved the loss of friendships that shaped my life as a girl.

I can't help but think of those dear friends when I read the story of Anna. She was a prophetess who, along with Simeon (who we mentioned in the last chapter), was present for Jesus' dedication as a baby in the temple, which was a Jewish custom. Anna was the final witness God brought to the event. She entered the God-orchestrated scene and added her thanksgiving to Simeon's prophecy and praise.

Luke describes her as "advanced in years" and mentions that she was married for seven years, then lived as a widow either "for" or "until" eighty-four years. The original language isn't clear, but she would have been at least 84 years old, and possibly 105!

There are only three verses about Anna in the Bible, but they are enough to establish her as an extraordinary woman of faith. Luke tells us she was a prophet of the tribe of Asher, and he describes her lifestyle this way: "She never left the temple but worshiped night and day, fasting and praying. Coming up to them at that very moment, she gave thanks to God and spoke about the child to all who were looking forward to the redemption of Jerusalem" (Luke 2:37-38).

Anna was a widow. In those days, if you didn't have a husband or children to care for you, you were forgotten and discarded by society. But God delights in using people the world thinks are nobodies. Interestingly, Anna was from the lost tribe of Asher. Most of Anna's tribe had been taken into captivity centuries ago. She could have been descended from a small group of exiles who returned from captivity. She was part of the believing remnant and a living emblem of God's faithfulness to His people.

Luke's description of her lifestyle may seem eccentric today, and it's likely it seemed that way in her time, as well. Her habits of worship, prayer, and fasting were a devotional routine, probably a lifestyle that spanned decades. She "never left the temple," which means she probably lived within the temple or on its premises, and she was always present, worshipping and serving God and the people who came to pray.

Every year in January, our church pushes the reset button as we all join in twenty-one days of prayer and fasting. Our church doors are open during certain times of the day, and we all fast from something in our lives: social media, caffeine, sugar, alcohol, or nicotine, for example. Every person chooses what they want to do, but the common thread is turning our focus to

God and gaining strength from Him as we begin a new year.

For me, fasting is pretty much a once-a-year activity, but Anna had made it a lifestyle. She was focused on God, and she had a hunger and thirst for His Word. She worshipped, praised, and honored Him every day, knowing that her prayer and fasting brought results. She was a special woman whose faith and faithfulness were seen by Heaven. I'm sure meeting Jesus, the Messiah, was the highlight of her life.

Anna had gone through tragedy, but she didn't become bitter. She didn't allow her loneliness or suffering to turn her inward. Instead, she found strength in her devotion to God. She was energetic, well-spoken, alert, spiritually savvy, generous, and unselfish.

As a prophetess, Anna received insight into things that were hidden from other people. That's why she was able to recognize who this child was, and it's why she shared the fulfillment of Scripture about the Messiah to all who would listen to her. She understood what Jesus meant for the people of Jerusalem, for she told everyone who was waiting for the redemption of Jerusalem that the Redeemer had arrived. She was one of several women mentioned in the Bible who played key roles in announcing the good news of Jesus' birth and, years later, His resurrection.

I remember receiving a prophetic word years ago that encouraged me greatly. It was after our church service one Sunday when it had been my turn to give the announcements. Upon dismissal, an older gentleman, who I later learned was referred to as "Brother Hoyt the prophet," came up to me. He held both my hands as he spoke these words over me: "You are a daughter of the highest King. He is doing and will do amazing work through you. You have a light inside of you the world cannot dim. You may think your work is finished, but you ain't seen nothin' yet. God is using you to reach the unreached. He has lit the path for you. Now you must follow His commands."

Tears were running down my face, and I think I almost blacked out at one point. He sounded like he was speaking in another language, and yet I understood every word. My mom happened to be attending church with me that day, and after Brother Hoy walked away, I sat down by her on the pew and wept. I couldn't believe such words were spoken over me. And yet, I could believe it. I knew God was working in my life, placing me in leadership roles in our church and requesting I rise to the occasion in my faith.

I understood through his words that God wanted me to keep my heart, motives, and purpose clear. Throughout my life, I had many times selfishly fought to advance my rank in my music career and business endeavors. But through Brother Hoyt, the Lord was asking me to step up and advance the Kingdom of God for His goodness, not my own. Maybe Brother Hoyt could see I was still clinging to leftover bits of selfish pride, or maybe God just used him to challenge my heart and remind me of His calling. Like Anna, he was "advanced in age," and with age comes wisdom and insight. His devotion to God enabled him to receive a divine message that I needed to hear.

Through Anna, we learn God can use any of us at any

age. You are never too young to follow Him wholeheartedly, and you're never too old. God is looking for people who are devoted to Him, people who love Him, listen to His voice, and share His words with those around them.

I pray you would always honor those older than you (even if do you poke fun at your mom and dad occasionally). Remember to heed the counsel of experienced Christ-followers whose trust in God has been a firm foundation that has sustained them for a lifetime. Their devotion and faithfulness have made them a well of wisdom, and you can draw advice and encouragement from their lives.

I also pray that you would live a life of devotion and fullness, as Anna did. You probably won't literally live in a church, but you can have the same commitment to God that she exemplified. You can place the same value on hearing and sharing His Word. Remember that someday, you'll be the "older woman" to someone else. That is probably impossible for you to imagine right now, but it's a beautiful thing. The outward signs of age—such as grey hair, wrinkles, and your own stories of the "good old days"—will be a sign of your inner strength and wisdom.

Never forget: whether you are young, old, or somewhere in between, God has both blessings and purpose for you today.

Love,

Mom

Woman at the Well

Timeless Grace

DEAR DAUGHTER,

THE OLDER YOU GET, THE LESS YOU LIKE TO ASK FOR HELP. I'll see you struggling to figure out a new toy, for example, and I'll offer to do it for you. But you refuse, insisting, "I can do it myself!"

I'm happy to see your independence, and I'm sure this is only the start. You are just hitting your tween years, so watch out, world! Strong girl coming through.

While independence is a good thing, it can also work against you if you don't learn when to recognize your need for help. Nobody can do everything, and even the strongest among us need mercy, grace, and assistance from time to time.

When I was nineteen years old, I was invited to go with a cousin of mine to a three-day spiritual retreat with a group of young women. At the time, I was getting ready to move my whole life to Tennessee, and I thought I had the world in the palm of my hand. This retreat seemed like a good opportunity to push the reset button before I set out on my own and made my dreams come true. I had been to several church camps before, and I knew I would enjoy the fellowship with other women. So I responded, "Sure, why not?"

We sang. We praised. We did Bible studies and went on nature hikes. Whatever it took to get in touch with God, you name it, we did it. It was a wonderful experience. On the final night, there was a time of worship, and then a speaker gave the closing message in the chapel at the center of the campus. When the message was coming to a close, I knew what would happen next. There would be a moment of invitation where those who needed prayer or who wanted to accept Jesus as their Savior would be called forward for prayer. That time was always exciting to me because I remembered the emotions of accepting Jesus in my heart at the age of eight, after my grandmother passed away. Since going to Heaven was a sure-fire way to get a ticket to be with her, I was in!

It came time for the closing invitation. But instead of those who needed God being called forward, they were told to remain in their seats. The leaders around them would lay hands on them and pray over them right where they were.

I felt like an old pro, secure in my walk with the Lord and somewhat self-righteous. People around me were praying and crying. Some were even speaking in tongues. I was looking around to see who I could pray for when suddenly I felt hands resting on my shoulders. People were going to pray for me! *Wait, what? Y'all, I'm good. I love me some Jesus.* I didn't need prayer, I assumed. I felt confident about where I was going after death. The moment was so awkward. I decided just to let them have their moment, though. If they thought I needed healing, well, go ahead and pray. It couldn't hurt.

The leaders were saying, "Give in, Charla. Release your burdens to the Lord." *Yeah, yeah. Okay, Sister Margaret. I'm ready to release my burdens and blow this joint.* But I just sat there, my head down, pretending to cry, until they finally moved on to someone else. It wasn't my most spiritual moment, that's for sure. I simply didn't think I needed help.

This memory didn't reemerge until years later when I read about a woman in the Bible whose name is never mentioned. She is usually known simply as the "woman at the well," and her story is found in John 4.

Jesus, traveling through Samaria on the way to Galilee, sat down at a well outside the town of Sychar. A Samaritan woman came to draw water from the well, and Jesus asked her for a drink. The woman was shocked. She asked Jesus how He could request this of her since she was a Samaritan and He was a Jew (the Samaritans and Jews didn't get along).

He replied, "If you knew the gift of God and who it is that

asks you for a drink, you would have asked him and he would have given you living water" (verse 10).

The woman pointed out that Jesus didn't have a rope or bucket, then she asked about this so-called living water. I'm sure she was being a little bit sarcastic.

JESUS WAS MAKING A POINT: THAT THE ENTIRE WORLD NEEDED THE GRACE OF GOD, AND HE WAS DETERMINED TO MAKE IT AVAILABLE.

Jesus then shifted the conversation. He began to tell her things about her life that He could not have known, including that she had been married five times and was not married to her current lover. The woman realized He was some sort of prophet or spiritual teacher, and she began to ask Him questions about God.

At one point, the woman said that she knew someday the Messiah would come. Jesus looked at her and said, "I, the one speaking to you—I am he" (verse 26).

This was the first time in the Gospels that Jesus directly stated He was the Messiah, and it was to a Samaritan woman. Jesus went out of His way to reveal Himself to someone who would be considered the lowest of society in that culture. He ignored the stigma around gender, race, and marital status. He talked to her directly, almost as equals, which shows His heart for all people, not just a few. Jesus was making a point: that the entire world needed the grace of God, and He was determined to make it available.

The woman ran off, leaving her water jar behind, and proclaimed to her entire village, "Come, see a man who told me everything I ever did. Could this be the Christ?" (verse 29).

Jesus didn't just heal the sick or disabled. He also healed the broken-spirited and the brokenhearted. This woman had sought validation in the attention of men. God knew her story, and He knew her heart. Even though she might not have realized it at the moment, she was in desperate need of healing.

I relate so much to her story as I look back on that moment of being told, "Release your burdens, Charla." I didn't think I had burdens to lay down. But I've learned that this is the way the devil works. He either shuts us down with shame or he puffs us up with pride. No matter how good our track record is in life, we still need the righteousness of Jesus.

I wish I could go back to that chapel pew, wrap my arms around my younger self, and say, "Honey, you don't have it all together like you think you do." If I could, I would tell the nineteen-year-old me that she desperately needs the grace of God, but first, she must ask for it. Living water cannot fill us unless we go to the source, and the only source is Jesus.

If I would have let go of my self-righteousness and given myself fully to God back then, maybe I could have avoided the pain of having to walk through so much darkness later on. I wasn't as holy, commit-

LIVING WATER CANNOT FILL US UNLESS WE GO TO THE SOURCE, AND THE ONLY SOURCE IS JESUS.

ted, or pure as I thought. I wasn't as clever and independent as I imagined myself to be. Perhaps if I could have recognized just how empty my life was, I wouldn't have tried to fill it with so many other things rather than running to the arms of the Father.

The woman at the well realized that Jesus had something to offer that she couldn't find anywhere else. See, she initially thought she needed water, but Jesus knew she needed life. The woman was smart enough and humble enough to accept His offer of salvation, and that changed everything.

After their conversation, she became one of the greatest messengers of grace in Scripture because, through her testimony, her entire village was saved. Jesus spent two days there teaching people about the love of God. It was a glorious, joyful ending that the woman could never have predicted when she set out for the well that day.

Even in your independence and strength, I pray that you would never lose sight of your need for grace. I pray that you would turn to Jesus for your satisfaction and fulfillment, not to a person, career, or passing pleasure. Jesus isn't there to condemn you or limit you, but to help you. To love you. To protect you.

Release your burden to the Lord, my precious daughter. He will carry it for you.

Love,

Mom

Mary & Martha

Timeless Faith

DEAR DAUGHTER,

SOMETIMES YOU GET FRUSTRATED BECAUSE YOU AREN'T OLD ENOUGH TO DO WHAT YOU WANT. You wish you could stay up later, or watch a particular movie, or go on the biggest ride at the amusement park, or have your own account on TikTok. I'm sure you think to yourself, *if only I were older, everything would be better.*

I understand. I really do. We all play the *if only* game at times. If only I had studied harder, I would have gotten a better grade. If only I had more money, I could buy the things I want. If only I had that girl's talent, I would be more popular or successful. If only I were prettier, that boy would fall in love with me. If only...

It never ends. There is always something that could've, should've, or would've happened. Sooner or later, we realize how futile that line of reasoning is. We can't possibly know what would have happened if things had been different. We shouldn't live with regret, wishing we could rewrite the past so our present would be something other than what it is.

This is where faith comes in. Faith isn't about what we can see, but what we can't see. We need faith because there is so much about life we can't see or understand. We don't know all the possible outcomes. We don't see all the dangers or opportunities or possibilities. But God does. Faith means we trust that God has guided us in the past, that His power is active in our present, and that our future will always be safe in His hands.

FAITH ISN'T ABOUT WHAT WE CAN SEE, BUT WHAT WE CAN'T SEE.

Mary and Martha, two famous sisters in the Bible, teach us about the need for faith. Mary, Martha, and their brother Lazarus were close friends of Jesus. Can you imagine being an actual bestie to the Messiah? I would have probably asked Him to bring forth a charcuterie board and turn water into wine too many times.

Jesus was a frequent visitor to their home. Luke recounts one memorable time when He stopped by their house. Martha was in the kitchen, stressed and flustered over meal preparations, while Mary sat at Jesus' feet and listened to his teachings. Martha finally couldn't take it. She complained to Jesus and asked Him to make Mary help her.

He replied, "You are worried and upset about many things, but few things are needed—or indeed only one. Mary has chosen what is better, and it will not be taken away from her" (Luke 10:41-42).

Mary chose Jesus over chores, and He commended her for that. Jesus reminded Martha that wearing a "busy badge" is less important than spending time with Him. In this short exchange, I immediately identify with Martha. I get so easily caught up in my day-to-day duties as a wife, mom, and business owner, I often forget to take even five minutes to spend time with God. But when I do, it changes my entire day. One word from God shapes my attitude and builds my confidence. I still face problems, of course, but my mind and heart are full of faith rather than full of myself.

Sometime after that story, Mary and Martha needed all their faith to face one of the greatest tragedies of their life: the sickness and death of their brother Lazarus. If you're familiar with the story, you know how it ends. Jesus raises Lazarus from the dead. It's a powerful, emotional story, especially because of the close relationship Jesus had with these siblings.

The sisters didn't have the benefit of being able to read ahead in their own story, of course. So when Lazarus became deathly ill, they were understandably upset. They sent a message to Jesus to come, saying, "Lord, the one you love is sick" (Luke 11:3). Jesus did not come immediately, which must have troubled the sisters. They had seen the miracles He did for other people. Why didn't He run to the rescue of one of His best friends?

Within a short time, Lazarus died. I can only imagine the grief and even anger that Mary and Martha must have felt. Not only was their brother gone, but now their livelihood was at stake with no one left to provide for them.

After Lazarus had been in the tomb for four days, Jesus finally showed up. Martha met Him outside the city. I imagine her approaching Him with arms flailing, voice trembling, and a bit of a snarky attitude. She said, "If you had been here, my brother would not have died. But I know that even now God will give you whatever you ask" (John 11:21).

Notice her *if only* mentality. If only Jesus had been there. If only Jesus had stopped this from happening. If only Jesus had cared enough to help. Who can criticize her? I would be saying the same thing. Why didn't you come earlier, Jesus?

Yet, there is a note of faith in Martha's voice, or at least of hope. "Even now, God will give you whatever you ask." She couldn't understand why Jesus had delayed His arrival, yet she hadn't given up on Him either. She knew Him too well. Maybe He had a plan.

It's interesting that Martha went out to meet Jesus, but Mary stayed in the house. I wonder if she was wounded and hurt. I imagine her heart was so broken that she found it hard to face even the Lord Himself.

Jesus asked Martha to get Mary. When she saw Jesus,

she said the same thing as her sister: "Lord, if you had been here, my brother would not have died" (verse 32).

The Bible says Jesus was deeply moved, and He wept for their pain. Then, He did something completely unexpected. He told them to remove the stone that sealed off the entrance to the tomb. Martha objected, saying that after four days, the body would smell.

I imagine Jesus smiling at her. Then He said, "Did I not tell you that if you believe, you will see the glory of God?" (verse 40). He said a brief prayer, then He called into the darkness of the tomb, "Lazarus, come out!" (verse 43).

Think of how silent everyone must have been. How they held their breath, peering into the tomb, wondering what to expect. Imagine the incredulous cheers and the abundance of tears that followed when Lazarus appeared, still wrapped in the grave clothes he had been buried in. It was one of the greatest miracles recorded in the Gospels.

One of my favorite speakers and authors, Bianca Juárez Olthoff, describes the moment this way: "Lazarus was dead, but he came back to life. Martha and Mary's faith was dead, and it came back to life."[4]

Jesus asks us the same question today: "Do you believe?" He wasn't just asking if they believed He could save their brother, but if they believed He was the Messiah, the

---

4 Bianca Juárez Olthoff, "Twelve More Women of the Bible Video Bible Study Online," Vimeo. (ThomasNelsonZondervan, December 8, 2016). https://vimeo.com/ondemand/womenofthebible/193892769.

living God who can bring forth life in all things. Can you do the same? In the midst of being bound by death and disappointment, do you firmly stand on your belief in Jesus? Even if everything has been ripped away from you, can you still worship God because you know He is good, He is able, and He can work miracles?

Saying "if only" means we focus on what we don't have, on what we didn't receive, on what we've lost. We look backward with regret. When we turn to Jesus, though, we look forward with faith. We focus on His goodness and power, and we put our trust in His will rather than in our ability (or lack of ability) to control our world.

Just as my music career in Texas began to build momentum, I was asked by a male artist to sing yet another duet with him. Our first collaboration had reached the top of the charts and was a roaring success. I was actively touring with him and his band in the promotion of our song together. We had formed a beautiful partnership. Yet, when he asked me to do another duet, I felt this pull in my gut that I needed to branch out on my own as a vocalist and performer instead of being regarded as the "girl who sings backup." I was determined to be more independent during that season of my career, and I made the tough decision to turn down his offer.

Here's where the gut punch came in and where the *if only* thoughts began to swirl. The duet he cut with another female artist went on to set chart-topping records and gross hundreds of thousands of dollars, not only in the Texas Music scene but also on mainstream radio. The girl who sang in the duet later became a country music mega-star, selling millions of records and touring worldwide.

For a long time, I beat myself up for having passed on the opportunity. I held bitterness and rebellion against God. I quit trusting my internal compass because I felt it had led me astray one too many times. If only I would have said

THERE IS NO WAY TO KNOW WHAT WOULD HAVE HAPPENED OR MIGHT HAVE HAPPENED. I COULD ONLY TRUST THAT GOD KNEW WHAT NEEDED TO HAPPEN,

yes, maybe I would have had the same explosive career. If only I wouldn't have listened to my gut, maybe I would have been on all the award shows, winning Grammys like her. If only...

Finally, after time passed, I concluded that "if only" was a dead-end street. There is no way to know what would have happened or might have happened. I could only trust that God knew what *needed* to happen, and He had led me down the right path. I had done my best to live wisely, with integrity and courage. The rest was in God's hands. Now it was time to walk in faith, trusting that God's ways were higher than mine.

That was what Martha and Mary had to do. The only way to find peace was to fall at the feet of Jesus and trust His plan. For them, His plan included resurrecting their brother from the dead, which was probably not a solution they could have foreseen. For me, it meant taking me down other career and family paths that I wouldn't trade for anything.

I look at my life now and thank the good Lord every day that I didn't pass up on all the incredible things I've been able to do. Things I would have never, in a million years, been able to accomplish if I would have had someone else's life. I would not have gone into radio, a career I immensely enjoyed. I probably would not have married your dad, who is a rock to our family. I wouldn't have had the opportunity to launch my business in the beauty industry and help countless others do the same. I would have never given birth to you, my precious daughter who brings sunshine to my cloudy days, or your brother, or have adopted your sister.

I pray that you would always be willing to trust God with everything. That you would believe He is a God who can heal, restore, resurrect, provide, protect, and bless. That you would love Him even if He doesn't come through the way you hoped, or when you are left with tiny fragments of faith after getting punched in the gut by life. I pray you would believe in the goodness and sovereignty of God, knowing that His plan is bigger and greater than your plans could ever be.

LET GO OF AN IF ONLY MENTALITY AND EMBRACE AN ONLY GOD MENTALITY.

Let go of an *if only* mentality and embrace an *only God* mentality. Only God can perfectly orchestrate all the moving pieces of your life. Only God sharpens you and prepares you for the blessings ahead. Only God can flip the script on your plans and bring about an even more fulfilling life in Him. God works all things together for good, as Paul writes in Romans 8:28. You just need to believe.

Love,

Mom

Mary Magdalene

Timeless Power

DEAR DAUGHTER,

S YOU'VE GROWN OLDER, THE IMAGINARY MONSTERS UNDER YOUR BED HAVE LOST THEIR POWER. The boogie man in the closet is a joke now, not an actual source of terror. I'm glad about that. Childhood fears should fade into oblivion as you grow up.

I have one fear that hasn't faded with time: mice. When I was growing up, we lived on the edge of town next to a cornfield. When the farmers would harvest the field, mice would make a beeline (or would it be a mouseline?) for our house. Then they would decide this new home was much safer than a cornfield, and they'd stay there.

I was never worried about monsters under my bed as a little girl. I was too terrified by the sound of mice scratching behind the walls. That memory still gives me the heebie-jeebies. To this day, I sleep with earplugs and a mound of pillows over my head, a leftover habit from my childhood trauma with mice.

Mary Magdalene didn't have mice in her walls or monsters under her bed. She had something much worse: demons controlling her life and body. The Bible tells us Mary Magdalene was a woman "from whom seven demons had come out" (Luke 8:2 NIV). The devil thought he had consumed her life completely, but the power of Jesus ended the years of torment she had endured with their fear, loneliness, darkness, and hopelessness. Her story teaches us that the only way to fight the power of evil is with the power of Jesus Christ.

After Mary had an encounter with Jesus, her life was forever changed. She was made whole. Her mind was sound, full of clear thoughts, no longer consumed by demonic torture. From that day forward, Mary Magdalene devoted her life to following Jesus. After having known darkness, Mary chose to be in the light. She became one of Jesus' most faithful and loyal followers.

You might think demons are mythical or only existed back in those times, but they are real, and they affect our lives even today. Demons aren't big, scary, gremlin-looking creatures, but rather they are negative forces of evil. I don't mean to get too spooky here, and I don't want to give the devil too much credit. We aren't supposed to go around all the time looking for demons or casting them out of strangers, so don't go overboard on this. But we can't ignore them either because the Bible teaches us that demonic powers will try to influence us in negative ways.

The term "spiritual warfare" is often used to refer to our fight against the work of supernatural evil forces. This isn't a fight we focus on all the time, and it's not something we do in our strength. Jesus is the one who gives us power over the Evil One. His name is our authority, and His victory is the basis for our prayers.

I learned about the power of Jesus to overcome the devil through a situation that was very close to our hearts: our foster care journey and subsequent adoption process.

The experience with the two foster baby boys was relatively smooth. They brought so much joy to our household, and we loved every moment with them. I can't express the privilege it was to pour into their lives during their stay with us.

JESUS IS THE ONE WHO GIVES US POWER OVER THE EVIL ONE. HIS NAME IS OUR AUTHORITY, AND HIS VICTORY IS THE BASIS FOR OUR PRAYERS.

The goodbyes were heartbreaking, though. I'll never forget your brother shouting at the CPS agent as she pulled out of our driveway with our second foster baby: "Give me my baby back!" It left me in a puddle of tears. We understood reunification was the goal, yet it never softened the blow to our souls after pouring so much love and care into a child. I don't care if it's two weeks or two years, there is a special bond that forms. It took your brother time to process letting go of that bond. I wasn't sure my momma's heart could take the pain. I knew God had called us to foster, but holy moly, it was hard on everyone!

Our hearts grew in the process as we loved each precious child of God, so we pushed through the pain and stayed the course. I learned so many lessons from you and your brother. I discovered you are more resilient than we ever imagined possible. You proved to be true warriors of faith throughout our fostering journey.

In January of 2020, we received a call from our agency. They were looking for an adoption-motivated family for a baby girl who had been left at the hospital months before, with no contact from either parent. She was with another foster family, but the agency wanted to transition her into a forever home.

We immediately went into a time of prayer and fasting for this baby girl, and we agreed to take her. Everything moved slowly because of the global pandemic, but after seven months of waiting, she arrived at our doorstep. She was an absolute angel. I cherish and honor her first foster family. It was clear they poured all their heart and soul into her. She was happy and healthy despite the prenatal drug exposure, a floppy airway, and cognitive concerns. She slept through the night like a pro, and we couldn't believe how regimented her routine was. She was a dream baby.

Then, she turned one year old. Endless teething pain altered her entire demeanor. For months, we were in and out of the hospital with visits for recurring ear infections, pneumonia, and respiratory issues. She went from the happiest baby in the world to a child beset with constant fussiness, whining, and sleepless nights.

We could feel the shift throughout our household. Our frustration manifested itself with yelling, crying, and hopelessness—and it was mostly me! I'm not proud of this, but I want to be honest: we started questioning if we were her forever family. Did she really belong with us if we couldn't meet her needs? Were we really the right fit for her, as we had felt so strongly when she arrived? I could feel the demons setting up shop in my own personality. The devil was hard at work, putting a strain on our marriage due to lack of sleep and impatience.

One night, deep in despair, I began to cry out to God for answers. As I rocked her back and forth, praying for her fever to break during yet another respiratory infection, I remembered the concept of spiritual warfare. Dear friends had shared stories of feeling under attack by the devil or of someone they knew struggling with internal darkness. That's when I felt God whisper, "Cast out the spirit of evil." At first, I pushed this thought aside. Then, I heard it again, "Cast out the spirit of evil."

I was desperate for a solution, so I chose to listen and believe God could work miracles. I rocked her back and forth and prayed, "God, we need you more than ever. This innocent child of yours is hurting. Her body is full of endless pain and suffering from past, unspoken traumas she's endured. She's facing negative energy, pain from birth, feelings of being unwanted, unheard, and unloved. Only Your power can defeat the power of evil inside her body. I pray You would fully restore her health. Bring back that happy, spirited child we met five months ago. Restore the love we held so deeply in our hearts. Darkness is not welcome here. We know only Your divine strength can rid her of these demons disguised as health issues. In Your holy name, amen."

I opened my tear-filled eyes. She looked up at me and smiled for the first time in weeks. Then, she drifted off into a deep sleep. I didn't know if my prayer reached the ears of God until the next morning. She and I both had gotten a full night of sleep. I couldn't believe how rested I felt. I sensed God not only cast demons out of her but out of my heart as well.

Slowly but surely, God healed our precious baby girl's body. We have only fought minor colds since that night. She is a true pleasure to be around. She's happy and loves to dance. I've watched a supernatural connection form between her and your dad, and my heart bursts wide open when I see how much they love each other. It hasn't always been an easy road, but after my casting-out-demons prayer, we found peace in knowing she was exactly where she was supposed to be: in our family.

There are different ways of looking at evil or describing the spiritual struggle of good and evil around us, so I'm not telling you what to believe about the devil or demons. But I do want you to know the power of God is real. He is stronger than any force of evil, any illness, any relational conflict, any addiction, any loss. He is stronger than death itself. We don't just serve a good, holy, and loving God, but a *powerful* God. He works on our behalf. Our lives are changed because we know Him.

Mary Magdalene was transformed when Jesus set her free. Maybe that's why she was so loyal to Him, even after His death. According to the gospels, after Jesus was arrested in the Garden of Gethsemane, the apostles fled and hid in fear. There was only one man specifically named who remained at the crucifixion, yet there were several women, including Mary Magdalene. These faithful women were willing to mourn at the foot of the cross to the very end, when Jesus took His last breath. It's hard to imagine the absolute, heart-wrenching agony they must have felt and the strength they had to embody to bear witness to the Messiah's death on the cross.

WE DON'T JUST SERVE A GOOD, HOLY, AND LOVING GOD, BUT A POWERFUL GOD.

Mary Magdalene was present when the lifeless body of Jesus was removed from the cross and carried to a tomb. It was Friday, and the following day was the Sabbath, a holy day. Mary and the other women planned to return to the tomb after the Sabbath to complete the burial process by preserving the body.

Sunday morning, before the sun even rose, Mary Magdalene was the first to arrive. But to her surprise, the tomb was empty and the body was gone. Fear and anguish filled her already broken heart as she ran to tell the disciples. They returned to see the tomb for themselves. They discovered that the clothes wrapped so carefully around Jesus' mangled body were now carefully folded and placed on the stone bench. The apostles left, but Mary stayed behind. She wept in devastation over what she assumed to be true: that the body had been removed or stolen.

At that moment, a figure appeared before her. I'm sure it would have been hard to make out who exactly it was through her eyes full of tears. Maybe it was a gardener or even the person responsible for moving the body of her Master. She pleaded with the figure to reveal where he had taken Jesus.

But then, the man spoke. "Mary," he said (John 20:16). That was the only word He spoke, but it was enough. There was no doubt about who was standing before her. Mary fell at His feet in joy and worship. Then Jesus told her to share the good news with the other disciples.

In this incredible encounter, Mary Magdalene became the first person to see the risen Savior with her own eyes. Even before He revealed Himself to the other apostles, Jesus appeared to a woman. In a time where women were looked down upon and not valued as equals, this powerful story teaches us that Jesus does not see us for our worldly credibility, status, race, or gender, but instead sees our faith and devotion toward Him. In the darkest moments, these women had stayed by Jesus, supported Him, cared for Him, even buried Him. Now, they were the first to celebrate His resurrected glory and power.

All of us go through dark moments when we feel sorrow and despair. Like Mary on Sunday morning, we may feel all hope is lost. But on that first Easter, Mary found the living, resurrected Messiah. He came to her just as the Savior comes to all who seek Him. When hope is lost and our eyes fill with tears, we too can hear our name called by a living God who knows our hearts. He brings light and joy, even in the darkest of days. Now, we can be witnesses of the living, resurrected Messiah and share the glorious news of the gospel.

I pray that you would always remember the power of God at work in you. I ask Him that you would resist evil, not in your strength, but in the strength of God, with the same power that raised Christ from the dead. I pray that the closer you walk with Jesus, and the longer you know Him, the more your life would be transformed.

You are called to be free, my daughter, and that freedom comes through the power of Jesus.

Love,

Mom

Bent Woman

Timeless Self-Confidence

DEAR DAUGHTER,

I **REMEMBER YOUR FIRST DAY OF SCHOOL.** You were nervous but excited as you walked through the doors and into a building that looked way too big compared to your tiny frame. I wanted to stay with you, but I also didn't want to be "that mom." You didn't want that either. Even though you were scared, even though you didn't know anyone else or have any idea what was ahead, you knew this was where you wanted to be.

Now, you're an old pro at school. You are already complaining about how "boring" it is and looking forward to when it's over. That's a long way away, my dear!

I'm sure there will be other times in your life when you walk into a room—a classroom, a locker room, a board room—and feel both nervous and excited, like you don't belong but you do belong at the same time. You'll look forward to what you are about to learn or accomplish, but you'll also wonder if you are up to the challenge. You might be painfully aware of your weaknesses or ignorance. You might worry about what other people think of you. You might question if you're in over your head. You might think that if people only knew who you really were, they'd laugh you out of the room.

But you won't let those thoughts stop you. You'll stay. You'll learn and grow. You'll take your seat at the table because you bring a lot to the table, and you are needed there. It might take a while for you to believe it or for other people to recognize it, but it will happen.

I was only five days into the launch of my beauty business when I had a maybe-I-don't-belong-here moment. My best friend had introduced me to this business opportunity, but I knew very little about it. I saw her excitement and jumped right in, mostly to support the dreams she had for her future. We lived four states away from each other, though, so I searched for other entrepreneurs in my area so I could learn more. It turned out there was a presentation taking place not too far from where I lived. I decided I'd better go and soak in as much information as possible if I wanted to succeed in my new venture.

I remember riding the escalator from the lobby of a grand hotel in Dallas up to a conference room. I entered through a pair of massive doors, then made my way down to the front row. I didn't know a soul there, but I decided to carry myself as if I had been in business for years. After all, if I wanted to earn my seat as a leader who belonged on the front row, I knew I'd better act confident, even though I was pretty much clueless. Acting confident while clueless is a skill I've honed over the years.

I'll never forget a precious lady who came up to me with a warm smile and said, "Welcome! We're thrilled you're here. So, who is your upline?"

I smiled back, trying unsuccessfully to hide my confusion. "Uh, my upline..." Long pause. "Jesus?"

I had little knowledge of the products and zero understanding of how the business model worked. However, I wanted to learn. I was eager to find out how I could not only grow my income, but eventually be up on stage, presenting like the leaders who spoke that night. Maybe it was because I had gained confidence in myself through my years of experience in music and radio. Or perhaps I was just tired of treading the waters of exhaustion, and I hoped this business could be my vehicle to a more stable place. I had been working myself into the ground for a long time, often for little income. I had heard stories of success and wanted a similar life for my own family.

A still, small voice of courage inside my heart propelled me past the awkwardness. It silenced the fears that I might not be good enough. I wanted to learn, grow, and succeed. There was a sense of desperation mixed with destiny inside my soul. So even though I felt a little intimidated and out of place, I stayed. And I'm so glad I did!

Maybe you've felt out of place a time or two in your life. That's completely normal—so don't let it stop you. God wants you to know that you are welcome in rooms and at tables where you might feel out of place. Other people might be slow to recognize that, but God sees it. He knows your potential and the gifts inside of you. Don't hang back just because you aren't the expert or you aren't perfect yet.

The Bible gives us a beautiful story of a woman who had every reason to feel intimidated but instead chose to be present. We don't know the woman's name, but we learn she had a debilitating ailment for eighteen years that seems to have caused her spine to be curved. One of my favorite women in ministry, Lisa Harper, describes her as the Bent Woman. Luke writes that she was bent over double and couldn't straighten up at all, painting the picture of a disability that brought much discomfort (Luke 13:11). My heart aches for her, as I imagine she was unable to stand in worship, do simple chores, wrap her arms around her family, or rest peacefully at night.

The woman must have heard that Jesus was teaching in the local synagogue that day. She was so desperate for healing and freedom that she would do anything to receive her miracle from Jesus. She must have exhausted all other options, but she knew that Jesus could set her free. She made her way to the synagogue and joined the crowd who was listening to Him teach.

This is where the story gets good. Jesus saw her, and His heart was stirred with compassion. He didn't ignore her. He didn't tell her to come back at a better time. No! He called her forward. Jesus wanted her to draw near to Him, even in her pain and suffering.

The woman must have been instantly terrified. What was He going to do? Blame her for her illness? Expose some hidden sin or past failure that was causing her pain? Tell her she didn't belong and expel her from the synagogue? Or was He going to heal her?

GOD WANTS YOU TO KNOW THAT YOU ARE WELCOME IN ROOMS AND AT TABLES WHERE YOU MIGHT FEEL OUT OF PLACE.

She had heard the stories of Jesus' power, but she also knew the judgmental, critical attitude of the religious people around her. She had probably been a victim of that for eighteen years.

Jesus didn't reject her or blame her. He simply said, "Woman, you are set free from your infirmity" (verse 12). Then He laid hands on her, and she was healed. A woman who had been bent over for almost two decades finally stood to her full height. She instantly began praising God for her freedom. The years of pain, limitation, and ridicule were over. She was made whole. She was free to realize her full potential.

Tears well up in my eyes when I see God's love in the exchange between Jesus and this bent-over woman. This is our Jesus. His arms are open to include us all. A woman whom others barely noticed was the center of His focus. She was used to being defined by her disability. But Jesus saw past that. He knew who she really was: a "daughter of Abraham" (verse 16) and a daughter of God. Other people saw the reasons she should be rejected, but He saw the reasons she should be brought near.

Sadly, her healing infuriated the synagogue leaders because it was the Sabbath, and they didn't think Jesus should heal on that day. You can hear the callousness and religiosity in the response of the leaders to the crowd: "There are six days for work. So come and be healed on those days, not on the Sabbath" (verse 14).

THIS IS OUR JESUS. HIS ARMS ARE OPEN TO INCLUDE US ALL.

Jesus called them out in front of everyone. "You hypocrites! Doesn't each of you on the Sabbath untie your ox or donkey from the stall and lead it out to give it water? Then should not this woman, a daughter of Abraham, whom Satan has kept bound for eighteen long years, be set free on the Sabbath day from what bound her?" (verses 15-16).

These leaders were more concerned about the protocol of their religion than the miraculous healing that had taken place before them. They tried to shut Jesus down and rebuke those who came seeking healing. Instead, Luke writes, "When he said this, all his opponents were humiliated, but the people were delighted with all the wonderful things he was doing" (verse 17).

Think for a moment about that word "bent." She was bent by her disability. Bent by a condition she thought was final. Bent by the loss of hope after so many years of torment. Bent by indifference and judgment and rejection. And yet, she bravely entered a room where she knew she might be criticized because she wanted to seek the face of Jesus. Her despair pushed her into her destiny.

Being "bent" is a powerful metaphor for how you might feel at times, especially when you have the opportunity to be in places of influence or growth. You can be all too conscious of the reasons you don't fit into the group or the criticisms people could have toward you. It's that feeling of nervousness mixed with excitement you felt on your first day of school—you can't wait to see what's ahead, but you're also scared because you don't know if you'll be enough.

More than likely, your self-doubt is not even telling you the truth. Psychologists use the term "imposter syndrome" or "imposter phenomenon" to describe the feeling people sometimes have that they don't deserve to be where they are or are not qualified to do what they are doing. People with imposter syndrome feel this way despite objective evidence that they *are* qualified and that they are doing a good job.

I'm not talking here about faking something or pretending to be someone you're not. I'm talking about knowing who you are, even if you still have a long way to go. About recognizing your worth, your potential, and your calling. About being willing to feel awkward while you learn and grow because you know that on the other side of awkwardness, you're going to find freedom. Sure, you'll be a little clueless sometimes. But cluelessness can be cured. Lack of self-confidence, however, will keep you silenced and bent forever.

Just as Jesus did with the bent woman, look past the reasons you *aren't* enough and see yourself as God does. Be willing to step out, to face ridicule, to be overlooked or outright rejected. Don't listen to those voices, especially if those voices are inside your head. Instead, believe in yourself. Well, believe in *Jesus* more than anything, but believing in Jesus includes believing that Jesus believes in *you*!

It's been over seven years since I told that sweet lady at the meeting in Dallas that Jesus is my upline. The funny thing is, that joking remark became a motto I've turned to many times over the years. I had no clue how to build a business, so I had to depend on God. I had to go to Him for courage, wisdom, and grace. And He came through. Jesus makes a great upline in all areas of life.

BELIEVING IN JESUS INCLUDES BELIEVING THAT JESUS BELIEVES IN YOU!

I should mention that I also studied a lot, asked tons of questions, went to events and conferences like that one in Dallas, and tried hard to learn from my mistakes. "Turning to Jesus" is more than just praying. If you have faith, it will show up in your actions. You might start out clueless, but you can't stay that way!

My point, though, is that often the biggest hindrance to success is not ignorance or inability but lack of confidence. This woman was bent over physically, but she was confident enough and desperate enough to push past the obstacles and find Jesus. Nobody would have blamed her if she had stayed home that day. But somehow, she knew she was created for more. That is so inspiring to me!

Over the years, I have had the opportunity to meet and coach women from all over the world. I'm not in ministry, but God has enabled me to use my business platform to minister to others by sharing His goodness through my story. I would never have met many of these women if it weren't for this business. They are beautiful, precious, capable women.

Some of them, like the woman in our story, are bent. Bent over in shame. Bent over from trauma. Bent over from failure. Bent over in despair from how their lives have turned out. Bent over because they lost sight of a God who delights in their abilities and their potential. I know because I've been there.

I've shared my story throughout these pages, and anyone who reads it can see that I've had my share of bent-over seasons. Some were due to my own mistakes, and some were imposed upon me by other people or life itself. I have often felt like an imposter. As my business began to grow, I didn't think I deserved to be successful. I didn't think people should take me seriously. I doubted my abilities and felt like a fraud. With my background in the radio and music industry, how could I have the gall to think I could be successful in a completely different business?

All these thoughts of being unworthy kept me bent over with anxiety and insecurity. I came to a place of paralyzing despair. My last-ditch effort was to draw near to God. I realized He had placed before me the opportunity to lead, and He had called and equipped me for that role. He helped me stand tall in my abilities, and He's using me to help others do the same. He has called me to foster confidence in the women on my team by nurturing a supportive community. God helped me see myself through His eyes, then He gave me the desire to be an encouragement to others. Together, we are building a community where the misunderstood can be understood and the silenced can be heard.

We need God to free us from the lies we tell ourselves. We are never too bent for divine healing.

I pray that if you are ever bent over, if you ever feel limited, silenced, forgotten, or insufficient, that you would turn to the One who can help you rise to your full potential. I pray you would hear the voice of God calling you toward the destiny He sees in you, which is far greater than what you see in yourself. Like the Bent Woman, God is calling you out of the crowd and bringing you forward. He is healing your soul and restoring you to your full height, your full potential, your bright future.

Believe in yourself the way God believes in you. Stand up straight and walk confidently through every open door He opens before you. The room won't be complete until you're in it. There is a seat at the table with your name on it. You've got this.

Love,

Mom

Priscilla

Timeless Generosity

DEAR DAUGHTER,

GRANDMA KIKI IS ONE OF YOUR FAVORITE PEOPLE IN THE WORLD. To the rest of us, she is Kim, but you called her KiKi when you were just learning to talk, and the name stuck. She is your dad's mother, of course, and my mother-in-law. Or, as I lovingly call her, my mother-in-*love*.

KiKi is a truly generous person. She was the first one at the hospital when you were born. When I was working a job that required me to leave by four o'clock in the morning, she would drive to our house before the sun came up. She would be there when you woke up, then get you ready for school so your daddy could head off to work as well.

KiKi is our go-to person if we have an urgent need. Even if it's the middle of the night, she is by our side at the drop of a hat. She never misses a birthday party, baseball game, dance recital, or talent show. She is always there with a shoulder to cry on or a timely piece of advice. Besides being a faithful wife and dedicated follower of Jesus, she is a living depiction of a generous, devoted woman.

When we dig into the life of Priscilla, an early church leader who appears several times in the book of Acts, we see similar characteristics to your grandma KiKi. Priscilla was not only a dedicated wife, but she was also a devout follower of God, a prominent leader in her church, and a mentor in the faith community. She was an influential leader and co-laborer with the Apostle Paul, and she was respected for her understanding of the gospel and her ability to share the Word with others.

She is mentioned six times in Scripture, each time together with her husband, Aquila. Apparently you couldn't separate the two of them: they were one. They were a team in their marriage, their ministry, and their business. Four out of the six times she is referenced in the Bible, her name comes before her husband's name. That may indicate she was more well-known or influential than he was. Not that it was a competition, of course, but in a culture where women were often treated as inferior or even invisible, it's encouraging to see the level of authority and grace that God gave Priscilla and to note how readily the church received her ministry. God does not limit our service or our gifts based on our gender. Priscilla is one of many examples in the Bible where we see women confidently exercising their God-given gifts and callings.

Priscilla must have been a multi-talented, high-energy person because she certainly wore a lot of hats. She and her husband were tentmakers, like Paul, which means she had a secular occupation (Acts 18:3). They also had a church that met in their home, which shows us that they were pastors (1 Corinthians 16:19). We see them actively instructing and teaching other people in Christian beliefs and doctrine, which illustrates their skill and knowledge in the faith (Acts 18:26). Finally, they traveled with Paul at times, ministering together with him (Romans 16:3). Talk about being a woman with excellent time management skills! We can learn a lot from Priscilla about how to juggle multiple responsibilities and callings with grace.

Priscilla was a woman who was strong and steadfast in her faith. So strong, in fact, that she put her life on the line for the apostle Paul. He told the church in Rome, "They risked their lives for me. Not only I but all the churches of the Gentiles are grateful to them" (Romans 16:4). At the end of his life and ministry, Paul honored Priscilla and her husband, showing his deep love for them and his gratitude for their ministry.

GOD IS LOOKING FOR PRISCILLAS TODAY: GENEROUS PEOPLE WHO ARE READY AND WILLING TO SERVE IN WHATEVER CAPACITY THEY CAN TO LOVE THE WORLD AROUND THEM.

Each time we read about Priscilla, she is in a different location. She could pack her bags and be ready to go at any moment. She didn't build her dream home up on a hill and spend the rest of her life on herself. No! She was willing to travel to wherever God called her to share the freedom found in Jesus.

God is looking for Priscillas today: generous people who are ready and willing to serve in whatever capacity they can to love the world around them and share the good news of Jesus. Generosity might include giving financially, but it's so much more than that. It's an ability to see beyond ourselves and a willingness to invest in other people.

Priscilla and Aquila remind me of two dear friends of ours, a married couple, who work in Africa with an organization called Real 4 Christ Ministries. We support their ministry financially, and their devotion to their marriage, their ministry, and their Lord inspires me every time I hear them speak. This couple works to build schools in remote parts of Kenya and to provide medicine, vaccines, and clean water to people in need. They will go anywhere they are needed to continue spreading God's love.

> YOU WERE CREATED TO BE GENEROUS BECAUSE GOD IS GENEROUS, AND WHEN YOU SHARE WHAT YOU HAVE WITH OTHERS, YOU REFLECT HIS NATURE AND HIS LOVE.

You don't have to travel the globe to be a Priscilla, though. You can start in your own home and community by lovingly giving to those around you in small, practical ways. Every smile, every kind word, every thoughtful deed is an act of generosity. You were created to be generous because God is generous, and when you share what you have with others, you reflect His nature and His love.

One of the greatest hindrances to loving other people is self-centeredness. I don't mean blatant arrogance, but rather a subtle, me-focused approach to life. We can get so wrapped up in our own needs, fears, and goals that we stop using our time and talents for other people.

When I landed an on-air personality position on the radio, I was a small fish in a big pond. I was in way over my head. I had no qualifications or experience, and yet God had given me a microphone and entrusted me with this newfound role. Thankfully, I was a quick learner, and our listeners were patient with me as I tried new things, even if I failed at a few of them.

While I loved my job and soon built rapport with my listeners, I remember feeling isolated in the sound booth from the other employees. Many of them had worked in radio for decades. To be honest, I got in my own head. I imagined them walking by the studio and saying, "Who does this girl think she is?" I built up their dismissive opinions so much in my mind that I hardly ever left the glass booth except for the occasional bathroom break, to avoid running into anyone.

One day, I finally had enough of my fear and self-centeredness. Here I was, a naturally social person who was in this role for a divine reason, and yet I was frozen at the thought of people seeing me as was unqualified. Rather than seeing how I could help and serve and give to others, I was hiding in a cocoon of insecurities. But enough was enough.

I decided to bravely step out from behind the mic and leave the vocal booth. I began to arrive at work early each day so I would have time to make the rounds to visit the sales staff, human resources, events staff, and upper management. I pranced around the building, chatting and spreading light to whoever would engage with me in conversation. I shared a smile with anyone who looked my way. I pushed past my comfort zone and served people right where God had placed me.

To my surprise, it wasn't as scary as I thought. People welcomed me with kind eyes and warm hearts. Some were sweet enough to compliment me on my on-air presence. Others gave me some much-needed constructive criticism. I not only developed strong bonds with my co-workers, but I also nurtured relationships that helped me become better at my craft. My goal was to share light with those around me, but they ended up pouring back into me, as well.

No, I didn't pack my bags and fly to a different country like our missionary friends. Walking across the street can be just as daring, though. And ultimately, it's the same principle of working hard to bless others rather than being consumed by self.

Priscilla teaches us to busy ourselves with love, not just the million-and-one things that vie for our attention. She shows us how to use our time, talents, energy, and gifts to bless and serve those around us. Priscilla was a hard worker, but her works were motivated by love and filled with grace. She knew God and she cared about people, so she dedicated her life to doing good. Rather than occupying ourselves exclusively with things that affect our lives, and instead of hiding inside cocoons of insecurity, we must continually look for ways to bless those around us.

Priscilla also teaches us to be faithful and reliable. She was a builder, a hard worker, and a brave companion. Her generosity translated into a solid work ethic. She wasn't ashamed of her "day job," and she wasn't afraid of hard work. Whatever our occupation might be, we can follow the example of Priscilla by being faithful in every area and doing our work with a joyful heart before the Lord.

Like Priscilla and your grandma KiKi, I pray you would be known in your circle of friends as someone who is generous and trustworthy. I pray that you would look beyond what you need or want, that you would see how you can serve people around you, and that you would use your talents and time to be a blessing. I hope you're a builder like Priscilla, a hardworking, high-energy, multi-tasking woman of God who lives her life from a place of love.

Judging by you and KiKi, generosity runs in the family. I'd say that's a great legacy.

Love,

Mom

Lydia

Timeless Blessing

DEAR DAUGHTER,

I LOVE THAT YOU ARE ALWAYS THINKING ABOUT YOUR FRIENDS. You listen to their ideas and find games you can all have fun playing together. You feel sad if one of them is sick or has a bad day at school. You often pray for them at night, especially if you know that someone is suffering.

I know that you love God, and I can see His love for others flow through you, even at your age. You have a heart that feels the pain of others and a mind capable of seeing things from their perspective. I know that your love will grow more and more as you get older. I know you'll discover the many ways God wants to use you to be a blessing to others.

The word "blessing" occurs throughout the Bible. It includes material blessings such as health and prosperity, but that's only part of it. The term has the idea of living with the peace, well-being, and favor of God. In the Bible, the focus is always on God. He is the ultimate blessing, and His presence brings us countless blessings. Some we can see, but many we cannot. Things like peace, love, joy, forgiveness, and freedom flow freely from God and fill our lives with blessings.

God has blessed us, and He calls us to be a blessing to others. My life motto is "Blessed to be a blessing." I know God didn't give me the story that I have just for me to keep it to myself. He hasn't changed me, shaped me, protected me, taught me, and poured out favor on me so I could turn inward, using my resources and experience just for me and ignoring needs around me. What an empty way to live! God wants me to use His gifts to help others.

An ancient entrepreneur named Lydia shows us the power of a life that is blessed to be a blessing. Lydia was the original #bossbabe. She lived in the city of Philippi, where she was the Vera Wang of her time, a seller of a unique, expensive purple fabric that would have brought her into contact with the rich and famous. She seems to have been highly regarded and prosperous, since she owned a spacious home and had household servants.

> IN THE BIBLE, THE FOCUS IS ALWAYS ON GOD. HE IS THE ULTIMATE BLESSING, AND HIS PRESENCE BRINGS US COUNTLESS BLESSINGS.

Even with her successful business, she made time for prayer and learning about God. That's how Paul met her. She was attending a prayer and Bible study group that met outside the city when Paul showed up and began sharing about Jesus. Lydia and some members of her household believed in Jesus and were baptized, and she immediately invited Paul, Silas, and their group to stay at her house.

Lydia was Paul's first convert on the continent of Europe. The little prayer meeting where she first believed eventually turned into a church. Later, after Paul left to continue his ministry in other places, he wrote the letter of Philippians to this community of believers. Lydia couldn't have known the significance of their initial meeting, but her instant hospitality played a key role in what would eventually become a thriving church.

I love how she used her resources and blessings to host Paul and Silas. She knew her resources could help spread the message of God's love. As soon as she heard God's Word through Paul, "the Lord opened her heart to respond to Paul's message" (Acts 16:14). She had a soft, open heart toward the Lord, and she was quick to respond to His Word. She was ready to give, ready to serve, ready to love. Her response included not only faith and baptism, but hospitality and generosity.

You'll have Lydia moments in your own life. Moments when you connect with God and realize He is pouring the love of the Spirit into your soul. Moments that fill you with a passion you can't contain, a desire to serve and give that spills over onto those around you. You'll find yourself in a position of influence, and you'll know that God has placed you there for a purpose.

I can't help but think that my years building a community of women through radio, music, sales, and other diverse businesses have not been just for my family or me, but they were preparation to serve more people than ever. To reach daughters of the Most High and to breathe life into their loneliness by guiding them to Christ. To remind them that friends may come and go, relationships may fade, family members may pass on—but we serve an eternal God who will shine a light in the darkness. I might help one person, or I might help millions. Only God knows. But if even one soul finds comfort and forgiveness through my faithfulness, I've fulfilled my destiny as a fellow daughter of the King.

God has blessed me through all my endeavors. Yes, there were some low moments and some missteps. Quite a few of them, actually. I've shared some of them in this book. If I had to sum it all up, though, I would say this: I feel *blessed*.

God has been good to me. And I know He's been good to you, too. He is not finished with any of us, so don't give up if you are going through a tough time. God will be faithful to His promises, and He will be faithful to you. You've seen His goodness, I'm sure, but there is a lot more of that goodness ahead!

God's goodness toward us is not meant just for us, though. It is always to share. His blessings are too great for us to grasp in closed fists. They can only be held in open hands, hands that are quick to share, ready to give, generous to all.

In my business endeavors, I strive to equip my team with the tools they need to be blessed to be a blessing to others as well. I introduce them to steps they need to take to grow their income and pay down debt. Once they are free from debt, they are encouraged to give back to their community.

GOD'S GOODNESS TOWARD US IS NOT MEANT JUST FOR US, THOUGH. IT IS ALWAYS TO SHARE.

That might be volunteering, starting a charitable organization, or contributing time or funds to existing foundations. I want them to see the power beyond a paycheck. I want them to recognize the impact they can have to touch lives beyond their immediate family. Over and over, I've watched people pay off credit card debt, student loans, medical bills, and even mortgages, then go on to share their blessings in countless creative ways. They find financial freedom to both live and give like never before. That's a true blessings breakthrough!

Being generous includes sharing the love of God and our faith in Jesus. His grace is the reason I've been able to endure all the challenges I've faced. Why wouldn't I talk about it? The Christian song "My Story" has a line that I love: "To tell you my story is to tell of Him."[5] Isn't that so true? Our lives always point back to God. I've received many messages thanking me for expressing my faith on social media. I'm not trying to sound

---

5 Big Daddy Weave, "My Story," Beautiful Offerings, 2015.

religious—I'm just sharing the things that have changed my life. Recently, one girl reached out to tell me about her friend who is suffering from ALS. It turns out that a simple how-to video I had posted about text replacement helped her communicate after she lost the use of her arms, legs, and fingers. But then, this friend with ALS read some of my other faith-focused posts on Instagram and began to ask the girl who contacted me about Jesus. It continually amazes me how God uses our small acts of generosity and faith to bless other people.

We can't take the credit for the blessings God has given us. Yes, we work hard, take risks, act wisely, get counsel, and so much more. But ultimately, even our ability and opportunity to do those things are gifts from God. Rather than being prideful, we should be grateful. And rather than being selfish with what we have, we should be generous with it.

What is the legacy you will leave behind? Building a business, buying a house, achieving financial security, or gaining fame cannot give you lasting happiness. They are beautiful blessings, but they are not the goal of life. Like Lydia, learn to step into all the blessings of God, never forgetting the source of those blessings, but instead using them to help heal a hurting world.

In the dedication of this book, I urged you to always be the sunshine God created you to be and to let His light pour over every person you encounter. I pray you would fulfill that calling. I hope you always hear God's voice deep within your soul, stirring you to love and generosity. I pray you would thank God for every blessing you receive and give His blessings away to people He places within your influence.

No matter how big you dream, God's dreams for you are bigger. No matter how much you give away, God gives you more. You can always turn to him, and you can always trust Him.

And remember, my sweet daughter, no matter where you go, or how old you are, or where God takes you, I'll always be here for you. You're the greatest blessing of all, and I love you.

Love,

Mom

CONCLUSION

IF THERE IS ONE THING WE LEARN FROM the diverse stories of women in the Bible, it's that each of us walks our own journey with God. There is no "right" way to be a woman, or a daughter, or a mother. The right way is simply to be *you*. It's to believe and trust and rest in His love, then to live your life to the fullest as you follow Him.

I find great comfort and inspiration in these biblical heroes, and I hope you have as well. Not just through their successes, but through their failures, weaknesses, and fears. At the end of the day, we are all human. We are all doing our best. We all need God. And we all live by faith and grace.

God is the only one who can give you the peace and joy your heart desires. He's the source of true fulfillment, security, and self-worth. His grace covers your mistakes and gives you hope for the future.

No matter what has happened so far or where you find yourself in life, God is reaching out to you now, reminding you of His life, and inviting you to walk with Him.

Dear Daughter, you are forgiven.
Dear Daughter, you are washed clean by the blood of Jesus.
Dear Daughter, your shackles are broken, and you are set free.
Dear Daughter, you are my gift and my light.
Dear Daughter, you are loved.

Love,

God

ACKNOWLEDGMENTS

To my spunky, talented daughter, Blake: you not only inspired this project, but you said many times, "Mommy, wake me up when you get up to write your book. I just want to sit with you. I'm so proud of you."

To my husband, Bryan: I couldn't have done this without your sacrifice by picking up the slack in our household when I was knee-deep in the writing process. You are my rock and my forever teammate in life.

To my son, Brax, and my daughter, Bristol: You are my motivation, and I can't wait to write a book of letters to each of you.

To my best friend, Hannah: thank you for daily picking up the phone to tell me how brave I am for sharing my truths.

To my writing coach, Jenn Day: this book would have never happened if you weren't there to hold me accountable and validate all the emotions that come with writing a book.

To my dear friend, Brandi Voth: thank you for introducing me to Jenn. This book would not exist without you connecting us.

To my early book readers, Cindye Foster, Rachel Henning, Elizabeth Brooks, Rheana Wilson, Sara Murrell, and more: you were in the trenches with me, helping with initial edits and bringing this book to life in an honest way. I'm forever grateful to God that He placed each of you in my life.

To my brother, Clayton: thank you for sharpening me and holding the highest standards in sharing my story.

To Mom and Dad: the lessons you've bestowed on my life are the reason I'm a mother who allows her children to explore creativity and independence so freely.

To the rest of my family and friends: thank you for allowing me to share glimpses of our lives together and inspiring so many stories within these pages. You've shaped the person I am today.

To powerful female speakers and authors like Gail Mays, Marian Jordan Ellis, Lysa TerKeurst, Jonalyn Fincher, Naomi Zacharias, Amena Brown, Jeanne Stevens, Bianca Olthoff, and Lisa Harper: thank you for you inspiring and shaping me. Your insights are reflected in this book.

To my seven nieces: I pray this book will be a guiding light into womanhood.

To Stephen Nutt, Brad Levens, and the rest of my Creekwood Church family: thank you for instilling in me a desire to help people become fully devoted followers of Jesus outside the church walls.

To my female business partners: may this book serve as a compass as you navigate the world of entrepreneurship.

To my editor, publisher, and friend, Justin Jaquith: your thoughtfulness and careful detail were exactly what this book needed to be carried to completion. I'm so grateful for all your hard work and kindness.

To my audio engineer and dear friend, Bart Rose: thank you for the hours of care you put into the audiobook. You are so talented.

To Jesus: thank you for walking alongside me as we wrote this book together.

To God: thank you for Jesus! I pray this book would touch many lives.

ABOUT THE AUTHOR

CHARLA CORN BARRETT is an entrepreneur, speaker, vocalist, and (now) author. Above all, however, she is a wife and the mother of three rambunctious children.

Charla has chased dreams from the flatlands of Texas to the promised land of Nashville and back to north Texas, where she became one of the Lone Star State's most well-known radio personalities. More recently, she started a highly successful cosmetics and skincare business that has grown into a force of its own. Her honest, humorous, and down-to-earth approach to life and the Bible will resonate with any mother or daughter looking to connect with God and her family.

Charla and her husband, Bryan, live in Fort Worth and are Texans through and through.